EVALUATING TRAINING PROGRAMS

EVALUATING TRAINING PROGRAMS

THE FOUR LEVELS

DONALD L. KIRKPATRICK

Berrett-Koehler Publishers
San Francisco

Berrett-Koehler Publishers, Inc.
155 Montgomery Street
San Francisco, CA 94104–4109
Tel: 415–288–0260   Fax: 415–362–2512

ORDERING INFORMATION

Individual sales. Berrett-Koehler publications are available through most bookstores. They can also be ordered direct from Berrett-Koehler at the address above.

Quantity sales. Special discounts are available on quantity purchases by corporations, associations, and others. For details, contact the "Special Sales Department" at the Berrett-Koehler address above.

Orders for college textbook/course adoption use. Please contact Berrett-Koehler Publishers at the address above.

Orders by U.S. trade bookstores and wholesalers. Please contact Publishers Group West, 4065 Hollis Street, Box 8843, Emeryville, CA 94662; 510–658–3453; 1–800–788–3123.

Printed in the United States of America

 Printed on acid-free and recycled paper that meets the strictest state and U.S. guidelines for recycled paper (50 percent recycled waste, including 10 percent postconsumer waste).

Library of Congress Cataloging-in-Publication Data

Kirkpatrick, Donald L.
   Evaluating training programs : the four levels / Donald L. Kirkpatrick.
     p. cm.
   Includes bibliographical references and index.
   ISBN 1–881052–49–4 (acid-free paper)
   1. Employees—Training of—Evaluation. I. Title.
HF5549.5.T7K569 1994
658.3'12604—dc20   94–32953
                                            CIP

First Edition
99 98 97 96 95   10 9 8 7 6 5 4 3

Book Production: Trinity Publishers Services
Composition: Classic Typography

To my wife Fern,
who has been my inspiration, helper, and encourager
through forty-plus years of happy marriage

Contents

Foreword

What is quality training? How do you measure it? How do you improve it?

If you ask these questions of training professionals, human resource professionals, and managers of business operations, they inevitably respond with:

"Meets customer needs . . ."

"Students learn what they are supposed to learn . . ."

"Right training, right person, right time, returning to a supportive environment . . ."

"Changes behavior . . ."

Wonderful words and great ideas! If you ask how your training operation is currently measured, the responses typically are:

"Money spent . . ."

"Number of people attending training (known as the "buns in seat" metric) . . ."

"Number of new courses built . . ."

"Number of training hours delivered . . ."

What you typically find in business training operations are the quantitative measures without the qualitative ones. What is needed is a blend between the two, where the training department is held accountable for both! Don Kirkpatrick's four levels of evaluation give you the ability to measure training quality correctly, accurately, and skillfully.

Within any quality system there are two sets of measures that one must respond to when assessing quality: the *internal drivers* that are used to measure your operation and the *external drivers* that your customers use to measure you. These quality measures are the driving forces behind quality improvements, as shown in Figure F.1.

Figure F.1. Quality Assessment Measures

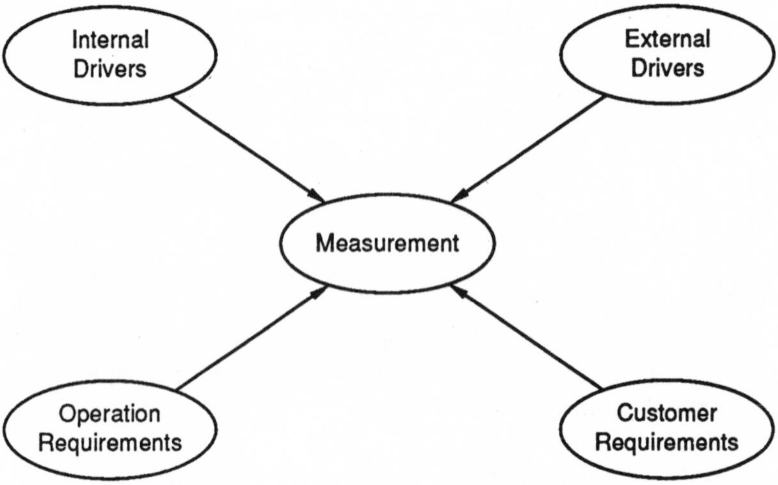

Within the framework of the Kirkpatrick model, level 1 and level 2 evaluation results are training departments' internal drivers. They provide the managers who run these departments with information on student satisfaction with the course and whether they have mastered the course content. Levels 3 and 4 then become the external drivers that provide information to business operations on the application of learned skills and on the impact on the business.

Systematically applied from course to course, with quality and improvement goals documented and measured, these four levels of evaluation can be used to assist training departments to become world-class operations.

So what does all this mean to your company? Motorola University and the Motorola training community use these levels of evaluation consistently to improve the quality of training throughout the world. You will see the same level 1 evaluation form being used in all situations, such as leadership training in Seoul,

Korea; operator training in Penang, Malaysia; six sigma quality training in Easterinch, Scotland; and senior executive training in Chicago, Illinois. You can observe testing of learned material in Austin, Texas; Hong Kong; Toronto, Canada; and Beijing, China. Finally, reviews on the application of skills are being conducted in Boston, Mexico, Singapore, and so on. In Chapter 12, you will find a case study describing Motorola's use of these levels.

So what does all this mean to you? These levels of evaluation can help you to make sound training investment decisions, they can help the training community to ensure that courses are working, they can help operations departments to identify barriers that are preventing skills from being applied, and they can help your company be confident that the hours your employees spend in training and the dollars that it invests in its people are time and money well spent.

Motorola believes that proper use of the four evaluation levels helps it to achieve its corporate vision of becoming the premier employer in the world by affecting our greatest competitive advantage — our people. It can do the same for you.

Dave Basarab
Manager of Evaluation
Motorola University

Preface

In 1959, I wrote a series of four articles called "Techniques for Evaluating Training Programs," published in *Training and Development,* the journal of the American Society for Training and Development (ASTD). The articles described the four levels of evaluation that I had formulated. I am not sure where I got the idea for this model, but the concept originated with work on my Ph.D. dissertation at the University of Wisconsin, Madison.

The reason I developed this four-level model was to clarify the elusive term *evaluation.* Some training and development professionals believe that *evaluation* means measuring changes in behavior that occur as a result of training programs. Others maintain that the only real evaluation lies in determining what final results occurred because of training programs. Still others think only in terms of the comment sheets that participants complete at the end of a program. Others are concerned with the learning that takes place in the classroom, as measured by increased knowledge, improved skills, and changes in attitude. And they are all right—and yet wrong, in that they fail to recognize that all four approaches are parts of what we mean by *evaluating.*

These four levels are all important, and they should be understood by all professionals in the fields of education, training, and development, whether they plan, coordinate, or teach; whether the content of the program is technical or managerial; whether the participants are or are not managers; and whether the programs are conducted in education, business, or industry. In some cases, especially in academic institutions, there is no attempt to change behavior. The end result is simply to increase knowledge, improve skills, and change attitudes. In these cases, only the first two levels apply. But if the purpose of the training is to get better results by changing behavior, then all four levels apply.

The title of the book, "Evaluating Training Programs: The Four Levels," is bold if not downright presumptuous, since other authors have described different approaches to the evaluation of training. However, in human resource development (HRD) circles, these four levels are recognized widely, often cited, and often used as a basis for research and articles dealing with techniques for applying one or more of the levels. For example, in the June 1993 issue of the ASTD's *Training and Development,* Shelton and Alliger wrote an article entitled "Who's Afraid of Level 4 Evaluation?" in which they quote my 1959 article in these terms: "In 1959, Donald Kirkpatrick proposed a four-level model of criteria for evaluating training: learner reactions, learning, job behavior, and observable results." Many other articles have referred to the four levels as the *Kirkpatrick model.*

I have used the word *training* in the title of this book, and I will use it throughout to include development. Although a distinction is often made between these two terms, for simplicity I have chosen to speak of them both simply as *training* and to emphasize courses and programs designed to increase knowledge, improve skills, and change attitudes, whether for present job improvement or for development in the future. Because of my background, my primary focus will be on supervisory and management training, although the concepts, principles, and techniques can be applied to technical, sales, safety, and even academic courses.

The book is divided into two parts. Part One describes concepts, principles, guidelines, and techniques for evaluating at all four levels. Selected references are provided at the end of Chapter 8. Part Two contains case studies from organizations that have implemented evaluation at one or more of the four levels. These case studies provide ideas and approaches for evaluating in other organizations.

I am grateful to Jane Holcomb for telling me that many trainers are looking for a first-hand description of the Kirkpatrick model and how it can be implemented and for suggesting that I write this book. I wish to thank those who have contributed to the book by writing case studies to illustrate the implementation of the four levels. I'm especially indebted to Dave Basarab at Motorola for both the Foreword and a case study. I'm also grateful to the American Society for Training and Development for permission to reprint Chapters 14, 19, 20, and 21. I also wish to thank the following people who reviewed the original manuscript and offered suggestions for improvement: Mike Fox, Scott Gassman, Matt Hennecke, Larry Lottier, Don McNeilly, Gary Sisson, Dick Swanson, and Virginia Treadway. Finally, thanks to Steve Piersanti, president of Berrett-Koehler Publishers, for his encouragement and editorial suggestions of a highly professional nature.

Donald L. Kirkpatrick

PART ONE

CONCEPTS, PRINCIPLES, GUIDELINES, AND TECHNIQUES

Part One contains concepts, principles, guidelines, and techniques for understanding and implementing four levels for evaluating training programs. Most of the content is my own and results from my Ph.D. dissertation on evaluation and my studies and experience since that time. Some modifications were made from the input I received from reviewers that fit in with my objective in writing the book: to provide a simple, practical, four-level approach for evaluating training programs. For those who want information on other principles and techniques, I have provided a selected reading list at the end of Chapter 8.

Chapter 1

Evaluating:
Part of a Ten-Step Process

The reason for evaluating is to determine the effectiveness of a training program. When the evaluation is done, we can hope that the results are positive and gratifying, both for those responsible for the program and for upper-level managers who will make decisions based on their evaluation of the program. Therefore, much thought and planning need to be given to the program itself to make sure that it is effective. Later chapters discuss the reasons for evaluating and supply descriptions, guidelines, and techniques for evaluating at the four levels. This chapter is devoted to suggestions for planning and implementing the program to ensure its effectiveness. More details can be found in my book, *How to Train and Develop Supervisors* (New York: AMACOM, 1993).

Each of the following factors should be carefully considered when planning and implementing an effective training program:

1. Determining needs
2. Setting objectives
3. Determining subject content
4. Selecting participants
5. Determining the best schedule
6. Selecting appropriate facilities
7. Selecting appropriate instructors
8. Selecting and preparing audiovisual aids
9. Coordinating the program
10. Evaluating the program

Suggestions for implementing each of these factors follow.

Determining Needs

If programs are going to be effective, they must meet the needs of participants. There are many ways to determine these needs. Here are some of the more common:

1. Ask the participants.
2. Ask the bosses of the participants.
3. Ask others who are familiar with the job and how it is being performed, including subordinates, peers, and customers.
4. Test the participants.
5. Analyze performance appraisal forms.

Participants, bosses, and others can be asked in : `erviews or by means of a survey. Interviews provide more detailed information, but they require much more time. A simple survey form can provide almost as much information and do it in a much more efficient manner.

A survey form, such as the one shown in Exhibit 1.1, can be readily developed to determine the needs seen both by participants and by their bosses. The topics to be considered can be determined by interviews or simply by answering the question, What are all the possible subjects that will help our people to do their best? The resulting list becomes the survey form.

As Exhibit 1.1 indicates, participants are asked to complete the survey by putting a check in one of three columns for each item. This is a much better process than having them list their needs in order of importance or simply writing down the topics that they feel will help them to do their job better. It is important to have them evaluate each topic so that the responses can be quantified.

After you tabulate their responses, the next step is to weight these sums to get a weighted score for each topic. The first column, *Of great need,* should be given a weight of 2; the second column, *Of some need,* should be given a weight of 1; and the last column, a weight of 0. The weighted score can then be used to

Exhibit 1.1. Survey of Training Needs

In order to determine which subjects will be of the greatest help to you in improving your job performance, we need your input. Please indicate your need for each subject by placing an X in the appropriate column.

Subject	Of great need	Of some need	Of no need
1. Diversity in the workforce— understanding employees			
2. How to motivate employees			
3. Interpersonal communications			
4. Written communication			
5. Oral communication			
6. How to manage time			
7. How to delegate effectively			
8. Planning and organizing			
9. Handling complaints and grievances			
10. How to manage change			
11. Decision making and empowerment			
12. Leadership styles—application			
13. Performance appraisal			
14. Coaching and counseling			
15. How to conduct productive meetings			
16. Building teamwork			
17. How to discipline			
18. Total quality improvement			
19. Safety			
20. Housekeeping			
21. How to build morale— quality of work life (QWL)			
22. How to reward performance			
23. How to train employees			
24. How to reduce absenteeism and tardiness			
25. Other topics of great need 1. 2.			

arrive at a rank order for individual needs. If two topics are tied for third, the next rank is fifth, not fourth, and if three needs have tied for seventh, the next rank is tenth. This rank order provides training professionals with data on which to determine priorities. Exhibit 1.2 illustrates the tabulations and the rank order.

The same form can be used to determine the needs seen by the bosses of the supervisors. The only change is in the instructions on the form, which should read: "In order to determine which subjects would be of greatest benefit to supervisors to help improve their performance, we need your input. Please put an X in one of the three columns after each subject to indicate the needs of your subordinates as you see them. Tabulations of this survey will be compared with the needs that they see to decide the priority of the subjects to be offered."

There will be a difference of opinion on some subjects. For example, in a manufacturing organization, the subject of housekeeping might be rated low by supervisors and high by their bosses. Other topics, such as motivation, will probably be given a high rating by both groups. In order to make the final decision on the priority of the subjects to be offered, it is wise to use an advisory committee of managers representing different departments and levels within the organization. The training professional can show the committee members the results of the survey and ask for their input. Their comments and suggestions should be considered advisory, and the training professional should make the final decision.

Participation by an advisory committee accomplishes four purposes:

1. Helps to determine subject content for training programs.
2. Informs committee members of the efforts of the training department to provide practical help.
3. Provides empathy regarding the needs seen by their subordinates.
4. Stimulates support of the programs by involving them in the planning.

The use of tests and inventories is another approach for determining needs. There are two practical ways of doing this. One way is to determine the knowledge and skills that a supervisor should have and develop the subject content accordingly. Then develop a test that measures this knowledge or skill, and give it to participants as a pretest. An analysis of the results will provide information regarding subject content.

The other approach is to purchase a standardized instrument that relates closely to the subject matter being taught. The sixty-five item Management Inventory on Managing Change (available from Donald L. Kirkpatrick, 1920 Hawthorne Drive, Elm Grove, WI 53122) is such an instrument. Here are some of the items in it:

1. If subordinates participate in the decision to make a change, they are usually more enthusiastic in carrying it out.
2. Some people are not anxious to be promoted to a job that has more responsibility.
3. Decisions to change should be based on opinions as well as on facts.
4. If a change is going to be unpopular with your subordinates, you should proceed slowly in order to obtain acceptance.
5. It is usually better to communicate with a group concerning a change than to talk to its members individually.
6. Empathy is one of the most important concepts in managing change.
7. It's a good idea to sell a change to the natural leader before trying to sell it to the others.
8. If you are promoted to a management job, you should make the job different than it was under your predecessor.
9. Bosses and subordinates should have an understanding regarding the kinds of changes that the subordinate can implement without getting prior approval from the boss.
10. You should encourage your subordinates to try out any changes that they feel should be made.

Respondents are asked to agree or disagree. Six other standardized inventories are available from the source just named: Supervisory

Exhibit 1.2. Tabulating Responses to Survey of Training Needs

In order to determine which subjects will be of the greatest help to you in improving your job performance, we need your input. Please indicate your need for each subject by placing an X in the appropriate column.

Rank order	Subject	Weighted score	Of great need	Of some need	Of no need
13	1. Diversity in the workforce—understanding employees	40	15	10	5
4	2. How to motivate employees	51	22	7	1
6	3. Interpersonal communications	48	20	8	2
18	4. Written communication	33	11	11	8
23	5. Oral communication	19	6	7	17
10	6. How to manage time	44	17	10	3
20	7. How to delegate effectively	29	9	11	10
20	8. Planning and organizing	29	6	17	7
14	9. Handling complaints and grievances	39	13	13	4
1	10. How to manage change	56	26	4	0

Topic						
11. Decision making and empowerment	1	5	24	53	3
12. Leadership styles—application	1	10	19	48	6
13. Performance appraisal	6	12	12	36	16
14. Coaching and counseling	2	20	8	36	16
15. How to conduct productive meetings	9	13	8	29	20
16. Building teamwork	0	5	25	55	2
17. How to discipline	1	11	18	47	9
18. Total quality improvement	4	13	13	39	14
19. Safety	2	13	15	43	11
20. Housekeeping	17	7	6	19	23
21. How to build morale—quality of work life (QWL)	2	6	22	50	5
22. How to reward performance	6	7	17	41	12
23. How to train employees	1	10	19	48	6
24. How to reduce absenteeism and tardiness	10	9	11	31	19
25. Other topics of great need					
1.					
2.					

Note: Tabulated responses from thirty first-level supervisors.

Inventory on Communication, Supervisory Inventory on Human Relations, Supervisory Inventory on Safety, Management Inventory on Time Management, Management Inventory on Performance Appraisal and Coaching, and Management Inventory on Leadership, Motivation, and Decision Making.

Many other approaches are available for determining needs. Two of the most practical — surveying participants and their bosses and giving a pretest to participants before the program is run — have just been described. Details of other approaches are described in my book, *How to Train and Develop Supervisors* (New York: AMACOM, 1993).

Setting Objectives

Once the needs have been determined, it is necessary to set objectives. Objectives should be set for three different aspects of the program and in the following order:

1. What results are we trying to accomplish? These results can be stated in such areas as production, sales, quality, turnover, absenteeism, and morale or quality of work life (QWL). Some organizations set objectives in terms of profits, even on return on investment (ROI). This is usually a mistake, because so many factors determine results like these that evaluation in these terms is often impossible.

2. What behaviors do we want supervisors and managers to have in order to accomplish the results? One such behavior is management by walking around (MBWA), the concept described by Thomas Peters and Robert Waterman, Jr., in *In Search of Excellence* (New York: Warner Books, 1982). All levels of management at United Airlines and Hewlett-Packard used this approach to show employees that they cared about them. The desired results are better quality of work life, higher morale, and thereby improved productivity.

3. What knowledge, skills, and attitudes do we want participants to learn in the training program? Some programs are aimed at teaching specific knowledge or skills. Others, such as programs on diversity in the workforce, are aimed at increasing knowledge and changing attitudes.

Robert Mager's book *Preparing Instructional Objectives* (Belmont, Calif.: Lake, 1962) describes specific concepts and approaches.

Determining Subject Content

Needs and objectives are prime factors when determining subject content. Trainers should ask themselves the question, What topics should be presented to meet the needs and accomplish the objectives? The answers to this question establish the topics to be covered. Some modifications may be necessary depending on the qualifications of the trainers who will present the program and on the training budget. For example, the subject of managing stress may be important, but the instructors available are not qualified, and there is no money to hire a qualified leader or buy videotapes and/or packaged programs on the subject. Other pertinent topics then become higher priorities.

Selecting Participants

When selecting participants for a program, four decisions need to be made:

1. Who can benefit from the training?
2. What programs are required by law or by government edict?
3. Should the training be voluntary or compulsory?
4. Should the participants be segregated by level in the organization, or should two or more levels be included in the same class?

In answer to the first question, all levels of management can benefit from training programs. Obviously, some levels can benefit more than others. The answer to the second question is obvious. Regarding the third question, I recommend that at least some basic programs be compulsory for first-level supervisors if not also for others. If a program is voluntary, many who need the training may not sign up, either because they feel they don't need it or because they don't want to admit that they need it. Those who are already good supervisors and have little need for the program can still benefit from it, and they can also help to train the others. This assumes, of course, that the program includes participatory activities on the part of attendees. To supplement the compulsory programs, other courses can be offered on a voluntary basis.

Some organizations have established a management institute that offers all courses on a voluntary basis. Training professionals may feel that this is the best approach. Or higher-level management may discourage compulsory programs. If possible, the needs of the supervisors, as determined by the procedures described in the preceding section, should become basic courses that should be compulsory. Others can be optional. The answer to the last question depends on the climate and on the rapport that exists among different levels of management within the organization. The basic question is whether subordinates will speak freely in a training class if their bosses are present. If the answer is yes, then it is a good idea to have different levels in the same program. They all get the same training at the same time. But if the answer is no, then bosses should not be included in the program for supervisors. Perhaps you can give the same or a similar program to upper-level managers before offering it to the first-level supervisors.

Determining the Best Schedule

The best schedule takes three things into consideration: the trainees, their bosses, and the best conditions for learning. Many times, training professionals consider only their own preferences and schedules. An important scheduling decision is whether to offer the program on a concentrated basis—for example, as a solid week of training—or to spread it out over weeks or months. My own preference is to spread it out as an ongoing program. One good schedule is to offer a three-hour session once a month. Three hours leave you time for participation as well as for the use of videotapes and other aids. The schedule should be set and communicated well in advance. The day of the program and the specific time should be established to meet the needs and desires of both the trainees and their bosses. Line managers should be consulted regarding the best time and schedule.

Selecting Appropriate Facilities

The selection of facilities is another important decision. Facilities should be both comfortable and convenient. Negative factors to be avoided include rooms that are too small, uncomfortable furniture, noise or other distractions, inconvenience, long distances to the training room, and uncomfortable temperature, either too hot or too cold. A related consideration has to do with refreshments and breaks. I conducted a training program on managing change for a large Minneapolis company. They provided participants with coffee and sweet rolls in the morning, a nice lunch at noon, and a Coke and cookie break in the afternoon. Participants came from all over the country, including Seattle. In order to save money on transportation and hotel, the company decided to take the program to Seattle, where it had a large operation. In Seattle, no refreshments were offered, and participants were on their own for lunch. Unfortunately, some peers of the participants had attended the same program in Minneapolis. These factors caused negative attitudes on the part of those attending. And these attitudes could have affected their motivation to learn as well as their feeling toward the organization and the training department in particular. Incidentally, more and more companies are offering fruit instead of sweet rolls and cookies at breaks.

Selecting Appropriate Instructors

The selection of instructors is critical to the success of a program. Budgets may limit the possibilities. For example, some organizations limit the selection to present employees, including the training director, the Human Resources manager, and line and staff managers. There is no money to hire outside leaders. Therefore, subject content needs to be tailored to the available instructors, or else instructors need to receive special training. If budgets allow, outside instructors can be hired if internal expertise is not available. The selection of these instructors also requires care. Many organizations feel that they have been burned because they selected outside instructors who did a poor job. In order to be sure that a potential instructor will be effective, the best approach is to observe his or her performance in a similar situation. The next best approach is to rely on the recommendations of other training professionals who have already used the individual. A very unreliable method is to interview the person and make a decision based on your impressions.

I recently conducted a workship for eighty supervisors and managers at St. Vincent Hospital in Indianapolis. I had been recommended to Frank Magliery, vice president of Operations, by Dave Neil of ServiceMaster. Dave had been in several of my sessions. In order to be sure that I was the right instructor, Frank attended another session that I did for ServiceMaster. He was able therefore not only to judge my effectiveness but also to offer suggestions about tailoring the training to his organization.

This is the kind of selection process that should be followed when you hire an outside consultant. It not only illustrates a process for selection but also emphasizes the importance of orienting an outside leader to the needs and desires of the specific organization.

Selecting and Preparing Audiovisual Aids

An audiovisual aid has two purposes: to help the leader maintain interest and to communicate. Some aids, hopefully only a few minutes long, are designed to attract interest and entertain. This is fine providing it develops a positive climate for learning. When renting or purchasing videotapes and packaged programs, take care to preview them first to be sure that the benefits for the program outweigh the cost. The extent to which such aids should become the main feature of a program depends on the instructor's knowledge and skills in developing his or her own subject content. Some organizations rely entirely on packaged programs because they have the budget but not the skills needed to develop and teach programs of their own. Other training professionals rely primarily on their own knowledge, skill, and materials and rent or buy videos only as aids. Some organizations have a department that can make effective aids and provide the necessary equipment. Other organizations have to rent or buy them. The important principle is that aids can be an important part of an effective program. Each organization should carefully make or buy the aids that will help it to maintain interest and communicate the message.

Coordinating the Program

I have experienced both extremes in regard to coordination. At an eastern university offering continuing education, I had to introduce myself, find my way to the lunchroom at noon, tell participants where to go for breaks, conclude the program, and even ask participants to complete the reaction sheets. I couldn't believe that a university that prided itself on professional programming could do such a miserable job of coordinating. The other extreme can be seen in a program that I conducted recently for State Farm Insurance in Bloomington, Illinois. Steve Whittington and his wife took my wife, Fern, and me out to dinner the evening before the program. He picked me up at the hotel to take me to the training room in plenty of time to set the room up for the meeting. He made sure that I had everything I needed. He introduced me and stayed for the entire program, helping with handouts. He handled the breaks. He took me to lunch and, of course, paid for it. He concluded the meeting by thanking me and asking participants to complete reaction sheets. He took me back to the hotel and thanked me. In other words, he served as an effective coordinator who helped to make the meeting as effective as possible. Of course, the niceties that he included are not necessary for effective coordination, but they do illustrate that it is important to meet the needs of the instructor as well as of the participants.

Evaluating the Program

Details are provided in the rest of the book.

As stated at the beginning of this chapter, to ensure the effectiveness of a training program, time and emphasis should be put on the planning and implementation of the program. They are critical if we are to be sure that, when the evaluation is done, the results are positive. Consideration of the concepts, principles, and techniques described in this chapter can help to ensure an effective program.

Chapter 2

Reasons for Evaluating

At a recent national conference of the National Society for Sales Training Executives (NSSTE), J. P. Huller of Hobart Corporation presented a paper on "evaluation." In the introduction, he says, "All managers, not just those of us in training, are concerned over their own and their department's credibility. I want to be accepted by my company. I want to be trusted by my company. I want to be respected by my company. I want my company and my fellow managers to say, 'We need you.'

"When you are accepted, trusted, respected, and needed, lots and lots of wonderful things happen:

- Your budget requests are granted.
- You keep your job. (You might even be promoted.)
- Your staff keep their jobs.
- The quality of your work improves.
- Senior management listens to your advice.
- You're given more control.

"You sleep better, worry less, enjoy life more. . . . In short, it makes you happy.

"Wonderful! But just how do we become accepted, trusted, respected, and needed? We do so by proving that we deserve to be accepted, trusted, respected, and needed. We do so by evaluating and reporting upon the worth of our training."

This states in general terms why we need to evaluate training. Here are three specific reasons:

1. To justify the existence of the training department by showing how it contributes to the organization's objectives and goals
2. To decide whether to continue or discontinue training programs
3. To gain information on how to improve future training programs

There is an old saying among training directors: When there are cutbacks in an organization, training people are the first to go. Of course, this isn't always true. However, whenever downsizing occurs, top management looks for people and departments that can be eliminated with the fewest negative results. Early in their decision, they look at such overhead departments as Human Resources. Human Resources typically includes people responsible for employment, salary administration, benefits, labor relations (if there is a union), and training. In some organizations, top management feels that all these functions except training are necessary. From this perspective, training is optional, and its value to the organization depends on top executives' view of its effectiveness. Huller is right when he states that training people must earn trust and respect if training is to be an important function that an organization will want to retain even in a downsizing situation. In other words, trainers must justify their existence. If they don't and downsizing occurs, they may be terminated, and the training function will be relegated to the Human Resources manager, who already has many other hats to wear.

The second reason for evaluating is to determine whether you should continue to offer a program. Some programs are offered on a pilot basis in hopes that they will bring about the results desired. These programs should be evaluated to determine whether they should be continued. If the cost outweighs the benefits, the program should be discontinued or modified.

The most common reason for evaluation is to determine the effectiveness of a program and ways in which it can be improved. Usually, the decision to continue it has already been made. The question then is, How can it be improved? In looking for the answer to this question, you should consider these eight factors:

1. To what extent does the subject content meet the needs of those attending?
2. Is the leader the one best qualified to teach?
3. Does the leader use the most effective methods for maintaining interest and teaching the desired attitudes, knowledge, and skills?
4. Are the facilities satisfactory?
5. Is the schedule appropriate for the participants?
6. Are the aids effective in improving communication and maintaining interest?
7. Was the coordination of the program satisfactory?
8. What else can be done to improve the program?

A careful analysis of the answers to these questions can identify ways and means of improving future offerings of the program.

I just talked to Matt, a training director of a large bank, and asked him to write a case history on what his organization has done to evaluate its programs. Here is what he said: "We haven't really done anything except the 'smile' sheets. We have been thinking a lot about it, and we are anxious to do something. I will be the first one to read your book!"

This is probably a typical situation, even in large companies. Most use reaction sheets of one kind or another. Most are thinking about doing more. They haven't gone any further for one or more of the following reasons:

- They don't give it a lot of importance or urgency.
- They don't know what to do or how to do it.
- There is no pressure from higher management to do more.
- They feel secure in their job and see no need to do more.
- They have too many other things that are more important or that they prefer to do.

In most organizations, both large and small, there is little pressure from top management to prove that the benefits of training outweigh the cost. Managers at high levels are too busy worrying about profits, return on investment, stock prices, and other matters of concern to the board of directors, stockholders, and customers. They pay little or no attention to training unless they hear bad things about it. As long as trainees are happy and do not complain, trainers feel comfortable, relaxed, and secure.

However, if trainees react negatively to programs, trainers begin to worry, because the word might get to higher-level managers that the program is a waste of time or even worse. And higher-level managers might make decisions based on this information.

In a few organizations, upper-level managers are putting pressure on trainers to justify their existence by proving their worth. Some have even demanded to see tangible results as measured by improvements in sales, productivity, quality, morale, turnover, safety records, profits, and even return on investment. In these situations, training professionals need to have guidelines for evaluating programs at all four levels. And they need to use more than reaction sheets at the end of their programs.

What about trainers who do not feel pressure from above to justify their existence? I suggest that they operate as if there were going to be pressure and be ready for it. Even if the pressure for results never comes, trainers will benefit by becoming accepted, respected, and self-satisfied.

Summary

There are three reasons for evaluating training programs. The most common reason is that evaluation can tell us how to improve future programs. The second reason is to determine whether a program should be continued or dropped. The third reason is to justify the existence of the training department. By demonstrating to top management that training has tangible, positive results, trainers will find that their job is secure, even if and when downsizing occurs. If top-level managers need to cut back, their impression of the need for a training department will determine whether they say, "That's one department we need to keep" or "That's a department that we can eliminate without hurting us." And their impression can be greatly influenced by trainers who evaluate at all levels and communicate the results to them.

Chapter 3

The Four Levels: An Overview

The four levels represent a sequence of ways to evaluate programs. Each level is important. As you move from one level to the next, the process becomes more difficult and time-consuming, but it also provides more valuable information. None of the levels should be bypassed simply to get to the level that the trainer considers the most important. These are the four levels:

Level 1—Reaction
Level 2—Learning
Level 3—Behavior
Level 4—Results

Reaction

As the word *reaction* implies, evaluation on this level measures how those who participate in the program react to it. I call it a measure of customer satisfaction. For many years, I conducted seminars, institutes, and conferences at the University of Wisconsin Management Institute. Organizations paid a fee to send their people to these public programs. It is obvious that the reaction of participants was a measure of customer satisfaction. It is also obvious that reaction had to be favorable if we were to stay in business and attract new customers as well as get present customers to return to future programs.

21

It isn't quite so obvious that reaction to in-house programs is also a measure of customer satisfaction. In many in-house programs, participants are required to attend whether they want to or not. However, they still are customers even if they don't pay, and their reactions can make or break a training program. What they say to their bosses often gets to higher-level managers, who make decisions about the future of training programs. So, positive reactions are just as important for trainers who run in-house programs as they are for those who offer public programs.

It is important not only to get a reaction but to get a positive reaction. As just described, the future of a program depends on positive reaction. In addition, if participants do not react favorably, they probably will not be motivated to learn. Positive reaction may not ensure learning, but negative reaction almost certainly reduces the possibility of its occurring.

Learning

Learning can be defined as the extent to which participants change attitudes, improve knowledge, and/or increase skill as a result of attending the program.

Those are the three things that a training program can accomplish. Programs dealing with topics like diversity in the workforce aim primarily at changing attitudes. Technical programs aim at improving skills. Programs on topics like leadership, motivation, and communication can aim at all three objectives. In order to evaluate learning, the specific objectives must be determined.

Some trainers say that no learning has taken place unless change in behavior occurs. In the four levels described in this book, learning has taken place when one or more of the following occurs: Attitudes are changed. Knowledge is increased. Skill is improved. Change in behavior is the next level.

Behavior

Behavior can be defined as the extent to which change in behavior has occurred because the participant attended the training program. Some trainers want to bypass levels 1 and 2—reaction and learning—in order to measure changes in behavior. This is a serious mistake. For example, suppose that no change in behavior is discovered. The obvious conclusion is that the program was ineffective and that it should be discontinued. This conclusion may or may not be accurate. Reaction may have been favorable, and the learning objectives may have been accomplished, but the level 3 or 4 conditions may not have been present.

In order for change to occur, four conditions are necessary:

1. The person must have a desire to change.
2. The person must know what to do and how to do it.
3. The person must work in the right climate.
4. The person must be rewarded for changing.

The training program can accomplish the first two requirements by creating a positive attitude toward the desired change and by teaching the necessary knowledge and skills. The third condition, right climate, refers to the participant's immediate supervisor. Five different kinds of climate can be described:

1. *Preventing:* The boss forbids the participant from doing what he or she has been taught to do in the training program. The boss may be influencd by the organizational culture established by top management. Or the boss's leadership style may conflict with what was taught.

2. *Discouraging:* The boss doesn't say, "You can't do it," but he or she makes it clear that the participant should not change behavior because it would make the boss unhappy. Or the boss doesn't model the behavior taught in the program, and this negative example discourages the subordinate from changing.

3. *Neutral:* The boss ignores the fact that the participant has attended a training program. It is business as usual. If the subordinate wants to change, the boss has no objection as long as the job gets done. If negative results occur because behavior has changed, then the boss may turn into a discouraging or even preventing climate.

4. *Encouraging:* The boss encourages the participant to learn and apply his or her learning on the job. Ideally, the boss discussed the program with the subordinate beforehand and stated

that the two would discuss application as soon as the program was over. The boss basically says, "I am interested in knowing what you learned and how I can help you transfer the learning to the job."

5. *Requiring:* The boss knows what the subordinate learns and makes sure that the learning transfers to the job. In some cases, a learning contract is prepared that states what the subordinate agrees to do. This contract can be prepared at the end of the training session, and a copy can be given to the boss. The boss sees to it that the contract is implemented. Malcolm Knowles's book *Using Learning Contracts* (San Francisco: Jossey-Bass, 1986) describes this process.

The fourth condition, rewards, can be intrinsic (from within), extrinsic (from without), or both. Intrinsic rewards include the feelings of satisfaction, pride, and achievement that can occur when change in behavior has positive results. Extrinsic rewards include praise from the boss, recognition by others, and monetary rewards, such as merit pay increases and bonuses.

It becomes obvious that there is little or no chance that training will transfer to job behavior if the climate is preventing or discouraging. If the climate is neutral, change in behavior will depend on the other three conditions just described. If the climate is encouraging or requiring, then the amount of change that occurs depends on the first and second conditions.

As stated earlier, it is important to evaluate both reaction and learning in case no change in behavior occurs. Then it can be determined whether the fact that there was no change was the result of an ineffective training program or of the wrong job climate and lack of rewards.

It is important for trainers to know the type of climate that participants will face when they return from the training program. It is also important for them to do everything that they can to see to it that the climate is neutral or better. Otherwise there is little or no chance that the program will accomplish the behavior and results objectives, because participants will not even try to use what they have learned. Not only will no change occur, but those who attended the program will be frustrated with the boss, the training program, or both for teaching them things that they can't apply.

One way to create a positive job climate is to involve bosses in the development of the program. Chapter 1 suggested asking bosses to help to determine the needs of subordinates. Such involvement helps to ensure that a program teaches practical concepts, principles, and techniques. Another approach is to present the training program, or at least a condensed version of it, to the bosses before the supervisors are trained.

A number of years ago, I was asked by Dave Harris, personnel manager, to present an eighteen-hour training program to 240 supervisors at A. O. Smith Corporation in Milwaukee. I asked Dave if he could arrange for me to present a condensed, three- to six-hour version to the company's top management. He arranged for the condensed version to be offered at the Milwaukee Athletic Club. After the six-hour program, the eight upper-level managers were asked for their opinions and suggestions. They not only liked the program but told us to present the entire program first to the thirty-five general foremen and superintendents who were the bosses of the 240 supervisors. We did what they suggested. We asked these bosses for their comments and encouraged them to provide an encouraging climate when the supervisors had completed the program. I am not sure to what extent this increased change in behavior over the level that we would have seen if top managers had not attended or even known the content of the program, but I am confident that it made a big difference. We told the supervisors that their bosses had already attended the program. This increased their motivation to learn and their desire to apply their learning on the job.

Results

Results can be defined as the final results that occurred because the participants attended the program. The final results can include increased production, improved quality, decreased costs, reduced frequency and/or severity of accidents, increased sales, reduced turnover, and higher profits and return on investment. It is important to recognize that results like these are the reason for having some training programs. Therefore, the final objectives of the training program need to be stated in these terms.

Some programs have these in mind on what we have to call a far-out basis. For example, one major objective of the popular program on diversity in the workforce is to change the attitudes of supervisors and managers toward minorities in their departments. We want supervisors to treat all people fairly, show no discrimination, and so on. These are not tangible results that can be measured in terms of dollars and cents. But it is hoped that tangible results will follow. Likewise, it is difficult if not impossible to measure final results for programs on such topics as leadership, communication, motivation, time management, empowerment, decision making, or managing change. We can state and evaluate desired behaviors, but the final results have to be measured in terms of improved morale or other nonfinancial terms. It is hoped that such things as higher morale or improved quality of work life will result in the tangible results just described.

Summary

Trainers must begin with desired results and then determine what behavior is needed to accomplish them. Then trainers must determine the attitudes, knowledge, and skills that are necessary to bring about the desired behavior. The final challenge is to present the training program in a way that enables the participants not only to learn what they need to know but also to react favorably to the program. This is the sequence in which programs should be planned. (See Chapter 11.) The four levels of evaluation are considered in reverse. First, we evaluate reaction. Then, we evaluate learning, behavior, and results—in that order. Each of the four levels is important, and we should not bypass the first two in order to get to levels 3 and 4. Reaction is easy to do, and we should assess it for every program. Trainers should proceed to the other three levels as staff, time, and money are available. The next four chapters provide guidelines, suggested forms, and procedures for each level. The case studies in Part Two of the book describe how the levels can be applied to different types of programs and organizations.

Chapter 4

Evaluating Reaction

Evaluating reaction is the same thing as measuring customer satisfaction. If training is going to be effective, it is important that trainees react favorably to it. Otherwise, they will not be motivated to learn. Also, they will tell others of their reactions, and decisions to reduce or eliminate the program may be based on what they say. Some trainers call the forms that are used for the evaluation of reaction *happiness sheets*. Although they say this in a critical or even cynical way, they are correct. These forms really are happiness sheets. But they are not worthless. They help us to determine how effective the program is and learn how it can be improved.

Measuring reaction is important for several reasons. First, it gives us valuable feedback that helps us to evaluate the program as well as comments and suggestions for improving future programs. Second, it tells trainees that the trainers are there to help them do their job better and that they need feedback to determine how effective they are. If we do not ask for reaction, we tell trainees that we know what they want and need and that we can judge the effectiveness of the program without getting feedback from them. Third, reaction sheets can provide quantitative information that you can give to managers and others concerned about the program. Finally, reaction sheets can provide trainers with quantitative information that can be used to establish standards of performance for future programs.

Evaluating reaction is not only important but also easy to do and do effectively. Most trainers use reaction sheets. I have seen dozens of forms and various ways of using them. Some are effective, and some are not. Here are some guidelines that will help trainers to get maximum benefit from reaction sheets:

Guidelines for Evaluating Reaction

1. Determine what you want to find out.
2. Design a form that will quantify reactions.
3. Encourage written comments and suggestions.
4. Get 100 percent immediate response.
5. Get honest responses.
6. Develop acceptable standards.
7. Measure reactions against standards, and take appropriate action.
8. Communicate reactions as appropriate.

The next eight sections contain suggestions for implementing each of these guidelines.

Determine What You Want to Find Out

In every program, it is imperative to get reactions both to the subject and to the leader. And it is important to separate these two ingredients of every program. In addition, trainers may want to get trainees' reactions to one or more of the following: the facilities (location, comfort, convenience, and so forth); the schedule (time, length of program, breaks, convenience, and so forth); meals (amount and quality of food and so forth); case studies, exercises, and so forth; audiovisual aids (how appropriate, effective, and so forth); handouts (how helpful, amount, and so forth); the value that participants place on individual aspects of the program.

Design a Form That Will Quantify Reactions

Trainers have their own philosophy about the forms that should be used. Some like open questions that require a lot of writing.

They feel that checking boxes does not provide enough feedback. Some even feel that it amounts to telling trainees what to do. Others keep it as simple as possible and just ask trainees to check a few boxes.

The ideal form provides the maximum amount of information and requires the minimum amount of time. When a program is over, most trainees are anxious to leave, and they don't want to spend a lot of time completing evaluation forms. Some even feel that trainers do not consider their comments anyway.

There are a number of different forms that can provide the maximum information and require a minimum amount of time to complete. Exhibits 4.1, 4.2, 4.3, and 4.4 show forms that can be used effectively when one leader conducts the entire program. Exhibits 4.5 and 4.6 show forms that can be used when more than one leader conducts the program and it is not desirable to have trainees complete a separate form for each. All can be quantified and used to establish standards for future evaluations. It would be worthwhile to try a form with several groups to see whether trainees understand it and whether it serves the purpose for which it was designed. All the forms illustrated in this chapter need to be tabulated by hand. They can be readily adapted so that they can be tabulated and analyzed by computer if that is easier.

Encourage Written Comments and Suggestions

The ratings that you tabulate provide only part of the participants' reactions. They do not provide the reasons for those reactions or suggest what can be done to improve the program. Therefore, it is important to get additional comments. All the forms shown in this chapter give participants opportunities to comment.

Typically, reaction sheets are passed out at the end of a program. Participants are encouraged to complete the forms and leave them on the back table on their way out. If they are anxious to leave, most will not take time to write in their comments. You can prevent this by making the completion of reaction sheets part of the program. For example, five minutes before the program

Exhibit 4.1. Reaction Sheet

Please give us your frank reactions and comments. They will help us to evaluate this program and improve future programs.

Leader _____   Subject _____

1. How do you rate the subject? (interest, benefit, etc.)

    _____ Excellent   Comments and suggestions:

    _____ Very good

    _____ Good

    _____ Fair

    _____ Poor

2. How do you rate the conference leader? (knowledge of subject matter, ability to communicate, etc.)

    _____ Excellent   Comments and suggestions:

    _____ Very good

    _____ Good

    _____ Fair

    _____ Poor

3. How do you rate the facilities? (comfort, convenience, etc.)

    _____ Excellent   Comments and suggestions:

    _____ Very good

    _____ Good

    _____ Fair

    _____ Poor

4. What would have improved the program?

Exhibit 4.2. Reaction Sheet

Leader _____   Subject _____

1. How pertinent was the subject to your needs and interests?

    _____ Not at all _____ To some extent _____ Very much

2. How was the ratio of presentation to discussion?

    _____ Too much presentation _____ Okay _____ Too much discussion

3. How do you rate the instructor?

	Excellent	Very good	Good	Fair	Poor
a. In stating objectives					
b. In keeping the session alive and interesting					
c. In communicating					
d. In using aids					
e. In maintaining a friendly and helpful attitude					

4. What is your overall rating of the leader?

    _____ Excellent   Comments and suggestions:

    _____ Very good

    _____ Good

    _____ Fair

    _____ Poor

5. What would have made the session more effective?

Exhibit 4.3. Reaction Sheet

In order to determine the effectiveness of the program in meeting your needs and interests, we need your input. Please give us your reactions, and make any comments or suggestions that will help us to serve you.

Instructions: Please circle the appropriate response after each statement.

	Strongly disagree	Agree	Strongly agree
1. The material covered in the program was relevant to my job.	1 2 3	4 5	6 7 8
2. The material was presented in an interesting way.	1 2 3	4 5	6 7 8
3. The instructor was an effective communicator.	1 2 3	4 5	6 7 8
4. The instructor was well prepared.	1 2 3	4 5	6 7 8
5. The audiovisual aids were effective.	1 2 3	4 5	6 7 8
6. The handouts will be of help to me.	1 2 3	4 5	6 7 8
7. I will be able to apply much of the material to my job.	1 2 3	4 5	6 7 8
8. The facilities were suitable.	1 2 3	4 5	6 7 8
9. The schedule was suitable.	1 2 3	4 5	6 7 8
10. There was a good balance between presentation and group involvement.	1 2 3	4 5	6 7 8
11. I feel that the workshop will help me do my job better.	1 2 3	4 5	6 7 8

What suggestions do you have for future programs?

Exhibit 4.4. Reaction Sheet

Please complete this form to let us know your reaction to the program. Your input will help us to evaluate our efforts, and your comments and suggestions will help us to plan future programs that meet your needs and interests.

Instructions: Please circle the appropriate number after each statement and then add your comments.

	High				*Low*

1. How do you rate the subject content?   5 4 3 2 1
   (interesting, helpful, etc.)

   Comments:

2. How do you rate the instructor?   5 4 3 2 1
   (preparation, communication, etc.)

   Comments:

3. How do you rate the facilities?   5 4 3 2 1
   (comfort, convenience, etc.)

   Comments:

4. How do you rate the schedule?   5 4 3 2 1
   (time, length, etc.)

   Comments:

5. How would you rate the program as an   5 4 3 2 1
   educational experience to help you do your
   job better?

6. What topics were most beneficial?

7. What suggestions do you have for future programs?

Exhibit 4.5. Reaction Sheet

Please give your frank and honest reactions. Insert the appropriate number.

Scale: 5 = Excellent 4 = Very good 3 = Good 2 = Fair 1 = Poor

Leader	*Subject*	*Presentation*	*Discussion*	*Audiovisual Aids*	*Overall*
Tom Jones					
Gerald Ford					
Luis Aparicio					
Simon Bolivar					
Muhammad Ali					
Chris Columbus					
Bart Starr					

Facilities   Rating _____   The overall program   Rating _____

Comments: Comments:

Meals   Rating _____   Suggestions for future programs:

Comments:

Exhibit 4.6. Reaction Sheet

The purpose of this conference is to help you. We need your reactions and comments to evaluate it. They will help us decide on the approach and content of future programs. Please use the following scale for your ratings:

5 = Excellent   4 = Very good   3 = Good   2 = Fair   1 = Poor

I. *Subjects and Leaders*

Subject	Rating	Leader	Rating	Comments
A. Manpower planning		Mason		
B. Technical training programs		Deady Horwitz		
C. Pattern for instruction		Fetteroll		
D. Audiovisual materials		Thomas		
E. Supervisory training		Morgan		
F. Trainee involvement		O'Brien		
G. Evaluation		Kirkpatrick		

II. *Other Aspects*

	Rating	Comments
A. Schedule		
B. Location		
C. Meeting facilities		
D. Food		

---

is scheduled to end, the instructor can say, "Please take time to complete the reaction sheet, including your comments. Then I have a final announcement." This simple approach will ensure that you receive comments from all or nearly all the participants.

Another approach is to pass the forms out at the beginning of the program and stress the importance of comments and suggestions.

Get 100 Percent Immediate Response

I have attended many programs at which reaction sheets are distributed to participants with instructions to send them back after they have a chance to complete them. This reduces the value of the reaction sheets for two reasons. First, some, perhaps even most, of the participants will not do it. Second, the forms that are returned may not be a good indication of the reaction of the group as a whole. Therefore, have participants turn in their reaction sheets before they leave the room. If you feel that reactions would be more meaningful if participants took more time to complete them, you can send out a follow-up reaction sheet after the training together with a cover memo that says something like this: "Thanks for the reaction sheet you completed at the end of the training meeting. As you think back on the program, you may have different or additional reactions and comments. Please complete the enclosed form, and return it within the next three days. We want to provide the most practical training possible. Your feedback will help us."

Get Honest Responses

Getting honest responses may seem to be an unnecessary requirement, but it is important. Some trainers like to know who said what. And they use an approach that lets them do just that. For example, they have the participants sign the forms. Or they tell them to complete the form and leave it at their place. In one program, the trainers used a two-sided form. One side was the reaction sheet. The other side sought attendance information: Participants were asked to give their name, department, and so on. I don't know whether the trainers were being clever or stupid.

In some programs, like those at the University of Wisconsin Management Institute, there is space at the bottom of the reaction sheets labeled *signature (optional)*. It is often meaningful to know who made a comment for two reasons: if the comment is positive, so you quote that person in future program brochures, or so that you can contact that person relative to the comment or suggestion.

Where people attend outside programs, they are usually free to give their honest opinion even if it is critical. They see little or no possibility of negative repercussions. The situation can be different in an in-house program. Some participants may be reluctant to make a critical reaction or comment because they fear repercussions. They may be afraid that the instructor or training department staff will feel that the reaction is not justified and there is something wrong with the participant, even that trainers might tell the participant's boss about the negative reaction and that it could affect their future. Therefore, to be sure that reactions are honest, you should not ask participants to sign the forms. Also, you should ask that completed forms be put in a pile on a table so there is no way to identify the person who completed an individual form. In cases where it would be beneficial to identify the individual, the bottom of the form can have a space for a signature that is clearly labeled as *optional*.

Develop Acceptable Standards

A numerical tabulation can be made of all the forms discussed and shown in this chapter. Exhibit 4.7 shows a tabulation of the reactions of twenty supervisors to the form shown in Exhibit 4.1. The following five-point scale can be used to rate the responses on a form.

Excellent = 5   Very good = 4   Good = 3   Fair = 2   Poor = 1

You tally the responses in each category for all items. For each item, you multiply the number of responses by the corresponding weighting and add the products together. Then you divide by the total number of responses received. For example, you calculate the rating for item 1, subject, as follows:

$$(10 \times 5 = 50) + (5 \times 4 = 20) + (3 \times 3 = 9) + (1 \times 2 = 2) + (1 \times 1 = 1) = 82$$

The rating is 82/20 or 4.1

You can use these ratings to establish a standard of acceptable performance. This standard can be based on a realistic analysis of what can be expected considering such conditions as budgets, facilities available, skilled instructors available, and so on. For example, at the University of Wisconsin Management Institute, the standard of subjects and leaders was placed at 4.7 on a five-point scale. This standard was based on past ratings. In this situation, budgets were favorable, and most of the instructors were full-

Exhibit 4.7. Tabulating Responses to Reaction Sheets

Please give us your frank reactions and comments. They will help us to evaluate this program and improve future programs.

Leader _Tom Jones_____   Subject _Leadership_____

1. How do you rate the subject? (interest, benefit, etc.)

   _10_ Excellent   Comments and suggestions:

   _5_ Very good

   _3_ Good   Rating = 4.1

   _1_ Fair

   _1_ Poor

2. How do you rate the conference leader? (knowledge of subject matter, ability to communicate, etc.)

   _8_ Excellent   Comments and suggestions:

   _4_ Very good

   _5_ Good   Rating = 3.8

   _2_ Fair

   _1_ Poor

3. How do you rate the facilities? (comfort, convenience, etc.)

   _7_ Excellent   Comments and suggestions:

   _7_ Very good

   _5_ Good   Rating = 4.0

   _1_ Fair

   _0_ Poor

4. What would have improved the program?

Note: Ratings are on a five-point scale.

time, professional trainers operating in nice facilities. In many organizations, limitations would lower the standard. You can have different standards for different aspects of the program. For example, the standard for instructors could be higher than the standard for facilities.

Measure Reactions Against Standards and Take Appropriate Action

Once realistic standards have been established, you should evaluate the various aspects of the program and compare your findings with the standards. Your evaluation should include impressions of the coordinator as well as an analysis of the reaction sheets of participants. Several approaches are possible if the standard is not met.

1. Make a change—in leaders, facilities, subject, or something else.
2. Modify the situation. If the instructor does not meet the standard, help by providing advice, new audiovisual aids, or something else.
3. Live with an unsatisfactory situation.
4. Change the standard if conditions change.

In regard to the evaluation of instructors, I once faced a situation that I'll never forget. At the Management Institute, I selected and hired an instructor from General Electric to conduct a seminar for top management. He had a lot of experience, both of the subject and in conducting seminars both inside and outside the company. His rating was 3.3, far below our standard of 4.6. He saw that we used reaction sheets and asked me to send him a summary. He also said, "Don, I know that you conduct and coordinate a lot of seminars. I would appreciate your personal comments and any suggestions for improvement." I agreed to do it.

I enclosed a thank-you letter with a summary of the comment sheets. My thank-you tactfully offered the following suggestions, which, I indicated, were based on the reaction sheets and on my own observations: "Use more examples to illustrate your points. Give the group more opportunity to ask questions. Ask your audio-visual department to prepare some professional slides and/or transparencies that will help to maintain interest and communicate."

I waited for a thank-you for my constructive suggestions. I am still waiting, and this happened in 1969. I did hear through a mutual friend that the instructor was very unhappy with my letter. He complained that he had taken time from a busy schedule to speak at the University of Wisconsin, he didn't take any fee or expenses, and the only thanks he had gotten was my letter. That was the last time he'd agree to be on their programs.

This example suggests that program coordinators should be very tactful in "helping" instructors by offering suggestions, especially if the instructors are members of top management within their own organization. One practical approach is to let instructors know ahead of time that reaction sheets will be used and that ratings will be compared with a standard. Instructors are usually eager to meet or beat the standard. If they don't, most will either ask for helpful suggestions or decide that someone else should probably do the teaching in the future. This is usually good news for the training staff, who may want to make a change anyway.

Communicate Reactions as Appropriate

Trainers are always faced with decisions regarding the communication of reactions to programs. Obviously, if instructors want to see their reaction sheets, they should be shown them or at least a summary of the responses. Other members of the training department should certainly have access to them. The person to whom the training department reports, usually the manager of Human Resources, should be able to see them. Communicating the reactions to others depends on two factors: who wants to see them and with whom training staff want to communicate.

Regarding who wants to see them, training staff must decide whether it is appropriate. Is it only out of curiosity, or does the requestor have legitimate reasons?

Regarding the desire of training staff to communicate the reactions, the question is how often the information should be communicated and in what detail. Those who make decisions about staffing, budgets, salary increases, promotions, layoffs, and so on should be informed. Also, as I suggested in Chapter 1, if there is an advisory committee, its members should be informed. If the concepts and principles described in Chapter 1 have been implemented, the reactions will be favorable, and top management will respect the training department and realize how much the organization needs it in good and bad times.

Summary

Measuring reaction is important and easy to do. It is important because the decisions of top management may be based on what they have heard about the training program. It is important to have tangible data that reactions are favorable. It is important also because the interest, attention, and motivation of participants has much to do with the learning that occurs. Still another reason why it is important is that trainees are customers, and customer satisfaction has a lot to do with repeat business.

This chapter has provided guidelines, forms, procedures, and techniques for measuring reaction effectively. Reaction is the first level in the evaluation process. It should be evaluated for all training programs. The responses to reaction sheets should be tabulated, and the results should be analyzed. The comments received from participants should be considered carefully, and programs should be modified accordingly. This measure of customer satisfaction can make or break a training department. It is only the first step, but it is an important one.

Chapter 5

Evaluating Learning

There are three things that instructors in a training program can teach: knowledge, skills, and attitudes. Measuring learning, therefore, means determining one or more of the following:

What knowledge was learned?
What skills were developed or improved?
What attitudes were changed?

It is important to measure learning because no change in behavior can be expected unless one or more of these learning objectives have been accomplished. Moreover, if we were to measure behavior change (level 3) and not learning and if we found no change in behavior, the likely conclusion is that no learning took place. This conclusion may be very erroneous. The reason why no change in behavior was observed may be that the climate was preventing or discouraging, as described in Chapter 3. In these situations, learning may have taken place, and the learner may even have been anxious to change his or her behavior. But because his or her boss either prevented or discouraged the trainee

Note: In the guidelines for levels 2, 3, and 4 no information has been given on how to use statistics. This subject is too complex to be included here. I encourage readers to consider statistical analysis. Consult people within your organization who are knowledgeable, and ask them to help you apply statistics to level 2 as well as to levels 3 and 4. Chapters 12, 13, 14, 15, 19, and 20 use statistics to determine the effectiveness of training.

42

from applying his or her learning on the job, no change in behavior took place.

The measurement of learning is more difficult and time-consuming than the measurement of reaction. These guidelines will be helpful:

Guidelines for Evaluating Learning

1. Use a control group if practical.
2. Evaluate knowledge, skills, and/or attitudes both before and after the program. Use a paper-and-pencil test to measure knowledge and attitudes, and use a performance test to measure skills.
3. Get a 100 percent response.
4. Use the results of the evaluation to take appropriate action.

The remainder of this chapter suggests ways of implementing these guidelines.

Use a Control Group If Practical

The term *control group* will be used in levels 3 and 4 as well as here in level 2. It refers to a group that does not receive the training. The group that receives the training is called the *experimental group*. The purpose of using a control group is to provide better evidence that change has taken place. Any difference between the control group and the experimental group can be explained by the learning that took place because of the training program.

The phrase *whenever practical* is important for several reasons. For example, in smaller organizations, there will be a single training program in which all the supervisors are trained. In larger organizations, there are enough supervisors that you can have a control group as well as an experimental group. In this case, you must take care to be sure that the groups are equal in all significant characteristics. Otherwise, comparisons are not valid. It could be done by giving the training program only to the experimental group and comparing scores before training with scores after training for both the experimental and control groups. The control group would receive the training at a later time. The example of test scores later in this chapter will illustrate this.

Evaluate Knowledge, Skills, and/or Attitudes

The second guideline is to measure attitudes, knowledge, and/or attitudes before and after the program. The difference indicates what learning has taken place.

Evaluating Increase in Knowledge and Changes in Attitudes

If increased knowledge and/or changed attitudes is being measured, a paper-and-pencil test can be used. (This term must have been coined before ballpoint pens were invented.) I'll use the Management Inventory on Managing Change (MIMC) described in Chapter 1 to illustrate.

Example 1 in Table 5.1 shows that the average score of the experimental group on the pretest (that is, on the test given

Table 5.1. Pretest and Posttest Scores on
the Management Inventory on Managing Change

		Experimental Group	Control Group
Example 1	Pretest	45.5	46.7
	Posttest	55.4	48.2
	Gain	+9.9	+1.5
	Net Gain	9.9 − 1.5 = 8.4	
		Experimental Group	Control Group
Example 2	Pretest	45.5	46.7
	Posttest	55.4	54.4
	Gain	+9.9	+7.7
	Net Gain	9.9 − 7.7 = 2.2	

before the program started) was 45.5 on a possible score of 65. The average score of the experimental group on the posttest (the same test given at the conclusion of the program) was 55.4—a net gain of 9.9.

Example 1 also shows that the average score of the control group on the pretest was 46.7 and that the score of the control group on the posttest was 48.2. This means that factors other than the training program caused the change. Therefore, the gain of 1.5 must be deducted from the 9.9 gain of the experimental group to show the gain resulting from the training program. The result is 8.4.

Example 2 in Exhibit 5.1 shows a different story. The net gain for the control group between the pretest score of 46.7 and the posttest score of 54.4 is 7.7. When this difference is deducted from the 9.9 registered for the experimental group, the gain that can be attributed to the training program is only 2.2.

This comparison of total scores on the pretest and posttest is one method of measuring increased knowledge and/or changes in attitude. Another important measure involves the comparison of pretest and posttest answers to each item on the inventory or test. For example, this is item 4 of the MIMC described in Chapter 1: "If a change is going to be unpopular with your subordinates, you should proceed slowly in order to obtain acceptance."

Table 5.2 shows that seven of the twenty-five supervisors in the experimental group agreed with item 4 on the pretest, and eighteen disagreed. It also shows that twenty agreed with it on the posttest, and five disagreed. The correct answer is *Agree,* so the positive gain was 11. Table 5.2 also shows the pretest and posttest responses from the control group. For it, the gain was 1. Therefore, the net gain due to the training program was 10.

Item 8 in Exhibit 5.2 shows a different story. Item 8 states: "If you are promoted to a management job, you should make the job different than it was under your predecessor."

Five of those in the experimental group agreed on the pretest, and twenty disagreed. On the posttest, six agreed, and nineteen disagreed. The correct answer is *Agree.* The net gain was 1. The figures for the control group were the same. So there was no change in attitude and/or knowledge on this item.

This evaluation of learning is important for two reasons. First,

Table 5.2. Responses to Two Items on
the Management Inventory on Managing Change

Item 4. "If a change is going to be unpopular with your subordinates, you should proceed slowly in order to obtain acceptance." (The correct answer is *Agree*.)

	Experimental Group		Control Group	
	Agree	Disagree	Agree	Disagree
Pretest	7	18	6	19
Posttest	20	5	7	18
Gain	+13		+1	

Net Gain   13 − 1 = 12

Item 8. "If you are promoted to a management job, you should make the job different than it was under your predecessor." (The correct answer is *Agree*.)

	Experimental Group		Control Group	
	Agree	Disagree	Agree	Disagree
Prestest	5	20	5	20
Posttest	6	19	6	19
Gain	+1		+1	

Net Gain   1 − 1 = 0

it measures the effectiveness of the instructor in increasing knowledge and/or changing attitudes. It shows how effective he or she is. If little or no learning has taken place, little or no change in behavior can be expected.

Just as important is the specific information that evaluation of learning provides. By analyzing the change in answers to individual items, the instructor can see where he or she has succeeded and where he or she has failed. If the program is going to be repeated, the instructor can plan other techniques and/or aids to increase the chances that learning will take place. Moreover, if follow-up sessions can be held with the same group, the things that have not been learned can become the objectives of these sessions.

These examples have illustrated how a control group can be used. In most organizations, it is not practical to have a control group, and the evaluation will include only figures for those who attended the training program.

It almost goes without saying that a standardized test can be used only to the extent that it covers the subject matter taught in the training program. When I teach, I use the various inventories that I have developed as teaching tools. Each inventory includes much of the content of the corresponding program. The same principles and techniques can and should be used with a test developed specifically for the organization. For example, MGIC, a mortgage insurer in Milwaukee, has developed an extensive test covering information that its supervisors need to know. Much of this information is related to the specific policies, procedures, and facts of the business and organization. Some of the items are true or false, while others are multiple-choice, as Exhibit 5.1 shows.

The training people have determined what the supervisors need to know. Then they have written a test covering that information. They have combined true-or-false statements with multiple-choice items to make the test interesting. A tabulation of the pretest responses to each item will tell the instructors what the supervisors do and do not know before they participate in the program. It will help them to determine the need for training. If everyone knows the answer to an item before the program takes place, there is no need to cover the item in the program. A tabulation of posttest responses will tell the instructor where he or she has succeeded and where he or she has failed in getting the participants to learn the information that the test covers. It will help instructors to know what they need to emphasize and whether they need to use more aids in future programs. It will also tell them what follow-up programs are needed.

This type of test is different from the inventories described earlier. Participants must know the answers to the questions in Exhibit 5.1. Therefore, those who take the test put their name on it, and they are graded. Those who do not pass must take further training until they pass the test.

In regard to the inventories, there is no need to identify the responses and scores of individual persons. The scoring sheet

Exhibit 5.1. Sample Items from a
MGIC Test to Evaluate Supervisor Knowledge

---

1. T or F   When preparing a truth-in-lending disclosure with a financed single premium, mortgage insurance should always be disclosed for the life of the loan.

2. T or F   GE and MGIC have the same refund policy for refundable single premiums.

3. T or F   MGIC, GE, and PMI are the only mortgage insurers offering a nonrefundable single premium.

4. _____   Which of the following is not a category in the loan progress reports?

   a. Loans approved

   b. Loans-in-suspense

   c. Loans denied

   d. Loans received

5. _____   Which of the following do not affect the MGIC Plus buying decision?

   a. Consumer

   b. Realtor

   c. MGIC underwriter

   d. Secondary market manager

   e. Servicing manager

   f. All the above

   g. None of the above

   h. Both b and c

   i. Both c and e

6. _____   The new risk-based capital regulations for savings and loans have caused many of them to

   a. Convert whole loans into securities

   b. Begin originating home equity loans

   c. Put MI on their uninsured 90s

   d. All the above

   e. Both e and c

   f. Both b and c

---

shown in Exhibit 5.2 is given to supervisors. They score their own inventory and circle the number of each item that they answered incorrectly. They keep their inventory and turn in the scoring sheet. These can be tabulated to determine both the total score and the responses to individual items. You can then use the resulting numbers as shown in Tables 5.1 and 5.2.

Exhibit 5.2. Scoring Sheet for the
Management Inventory on Managing Change

Management Inventory on Managing Change   Date _____

Please circle by number those items you answered incorrectly according to the scoring key. Then determine your score by subtracting the number wrong from 65.

1	2	3	4	5	6	7	8	9	10	11	12	13	14	15	16	17	18
19	20	21	22	23	24	25	26	27	28	29	30	31	32	33	34
35	36	37	38	39	40	41	42	43	44	45	46	47	48	49	50
51	52	53	54	55	56	57	58	59	60	61	62	63	64	65

Score   65 −   =

Both the MIMC and the MGIC examples are typical of efforts to measure increase in knowledge and/or changes in attitudes.

Evaluating Increase in Skills

If the objective of a program is to increase the skills of participants, then a performance test is needed. For example, some programs aim at improving oral communication skills. A trained instructor can evaluate the level of proficiency. Other participants may also be qualified if they have been given standards of performance. For the pretest, you can have each person give a short talk before any training has been given. The instructor can measure these talks and assign them a grade. During the program, the instructor provides principles and techniques for making an effective talk. The increase in skills can be measured for each succeeding talk that participants give. The same approach can be used to measure such skills as writing, conducting meetings, and conducting performance appraisal interviews.

The same principles and techniques apply when technical skills, such as using a computer, making out forms, and selling, are taught. Of course, the before-and-after approach is not necessary where the learner has no previous skill. An evaluation of the skill after instruction measures the learning that has taken place.

Get a 100 Percent Response

Anything less than a 100 percent response requires a carefully designed approach to select a sample group and analyze the results statistically. It is not difficult to get everyone in the group to participate, and tabulations become simple. Tables 5.1 and 5.2 show how this can be done. It is desirable to analyze the tabulations shown in Tables 5.1 and 5.2 statistically, but in most organizations it is not necessary.

Take Appropriate Action

There is an old saying that, if the learner hasn't learned, the teacher hasn't taught. This is a good philosophy for each instructor to have. It is only too easy to blame a learner for not learning. How many times have we trainers said (or perhaps only thought) to someone whom we are teaching, "How many times do I have to tell you before you catch on?" And usually the tone makes it clear that we are criticizing the learner, not simply asking a question. Another old saying applies pretty well to the same situation: When you point a finger at another person, you are pointing three fingers at yourself! This saying, too, can be applied in many teaching situations.

The important point is that we are measuring our own effectiveness as instructors when we evaluate participants' learning. If we haven't succeeded, let's look at ourselves and ask where we have failed, not what is the matter with the learners. And if we discover that we have not been successful instructors, let's figure how we can be more effective in the future. Sometimes the answer is simply better preparation. Sometimes it's the use of aids that help us to maintain interest and communicate more effectively. And sometimes the answer is to replace the instructor.

Summary

Evaluating learning is important. Without learning, no change in behavior will occur. Sometimes, the learning objective is to increase knowledge. Increased knowledge is relatively easy to measure by means of a test related to the content of the program that we administer before and after the training. If the knowledge is new, there is no need for a pretest. But if we are teaching concepts, principles, and techniques that trainees may already know, a pretest that we can compare with a posttest is necessary.

We can measure attitudes with a paper-and-pencil test. For example, programs on diversity in the workforce aim primarily at changing attitudes. We can design an attitude survey that covers the attitudes we want participants to have after taking part in the program. A comparison of the results from before and after training can indicate what changes have taken place. In such cases, it is important not to identify learners so we can be sure that they will give honest answers, not the answers that we want them to give.

The third thing that can be learned is skills. In these situations, a performance test is necessary. A pretest will be necessary if it is possible that they already possess some of the skills taught. If you are teaching something entirely new, then the posttest alone will measure the extent to which they have learned the skill.

Chapter 6

Evaluating Behavior

What happens when trainees leave the classroom and return to their jobs? How much transfer of knowledge, skills, and attitudes occurs? That is what level 3 attempts to evaluate. In other words, what change in job behavior occurred because people attended a training program?

It is obvious that this question is more complicated and difficult to answer than evaluating at the first two levels. First, trainees cannot change their behavior until they have an opportunity to do so. For example, if you, the reader of this book, decide to use some of the principles and techniques that I have described, you must wait until you have a training program to evaluate. Likewise, if the training program is designed to teach a person how to conduct an effective performance appraisal interview, the trainee cannot apply the learning until an interview is held.

Second, it is impossible to predict when a change in behavior will occur. Even if a trainee has an opportunity to apply the learning, he or she may not do it immediately. In fact, change in behavior may occur at any time after the first opportunity, or it may never occur.

Third, the trainee may apply the learning to the job and come to one of the following conclusions: "I like what happened, and I plan to continue to use the new behavior." "I don't like what happened, and I will go back to my old behavior." "I like what happened, but the boss and/or time restraints prevent me from continuing it." We all hope that the rewards for changing behavior will cause the trainee to come to the first of these conclusions. It is important, therefore, to provide help, encouragement, and rewards when the trainee returns to the job from the training class. One type of reward is intrinsic. This term refers to the inward feelings of satisfaction, pride, achievement, and happiness that can occur when the new behavior is used. Extrinsic rewards are also important. These are the rewards that come from the outside. They include praise, increased freedom and empowerment, merit pay increases, and other forms of recognition that come as the result of the change in behavior.

In regard to reaction and learning, the evaluation can and should take place immediately. When you evaluate change in behavior, you have to make some important decisions: when to evaluate, how often to evaluate, and how to evaluate. This makes it more time-consuming and difficult to do than levels 1 and 2. Here are some guidelines to follow when evaluating at level 3.

Guidelines for Evaluating Behavior

1. Use a control group if practical.
2. Allow time for behavior change to take place.
3. Evaluate both before and after the program if practical.
4. Survey and/or interview one or more of the following: trainees, their immediate supervisor, their subordinates, and others who often observe their behavior.
5. Get 100 percent response or a sampling.
6. Repeat the evaluation at appropriate times.
7. Consider cost versus benefits.

The remainder of this chapter suggests ways of implementing these guidelines.

Use a Control Group If Practical

Chapter 5 described the use of control groups in detail. A comparison of the change in behavior of a control group with the change experienced by the experimental group can add evidence that the change in behavior occurred because of the training program and not for other reasons. However, caution must be taken to be sure the two groups are equal in all factors that could have an effect on behavior. This may be difficult if not impossible to do.

Allow Time for Behavior Change to Take Place

As already indicated, no evaluation should be attempted until trainees have had an opportunity to use the new behavior. Sometimes, there is an immediate opportunity for applying it on the job. For example, if the training program is trying to change attitudes toward certain subordinates by teaching about diversity in the workforce, participants have an immediate opportunity to change attitudes and behavior as soon as they return to the job. Or if the program teaches management by walking around (MBWA), as encouraged by United Airlines and Hewlett-Packard, participants have an opportunity to use the technique right away. However, if the purpose of the training is to teach a foreman how to handle a grievance, no change in behavior is possible until a grievance has been filed.

Even if a participant has an immediate opportunity to transfer the training to the job, you should still allow some time for this transfer to occur. For some programs, two or three months after training is a good rule of thumb. For others, six months is more realistic. Be sure to give trainees time to get back to the job, consider the new suggested behavior, and try it out.

Evaluate Both Before and After the Program If Practical

Sometimes evaluation before and after a program is practical, and sometimes it is not even possible. For example, supervisors who attend the University of Wisconsin Management Institute training programs sometimes do not enroll until a day or two before the program starts. It would not be possible for the instructors or designated research students to measure their behavior before the program. In an in-house program, it would be possible, but it might not be practical because of time and budget constraints.

It is important when planning a supervisory training program to determine the kind of behavior that supervisors should have in order to be most effective. Before the training program, you measure the behavior of the supervisors. After the program, at a time to be determined as just outlined, you measure the behavior of the supervisors again to see whether any change has taken place in relation to the knowledge, skills, and/or attitudes that the training program taught. By comparing the behaviors observed before and after the program, you can determine any change that has taken place.

An alternative approach can also be effective. Under this approach, you measure behavior after the program only. Those whom you interview or survey are asked to identify any behavior that was different than it had been before the program. This was the approach that we used at the Management Institute to evaluate the three-day supervisory training program called Developing Supervisory Skills. Chapter 17 describes this evaluation.

In some cases, the training professionals and/or persons whom they select can observe the behavior personally.

Survey and/or Interview
Persons Who Know the Behavior

As the guideline suggests, evaluators should survey and/or interview one or more of the following: trainees, their immediate supervisor, their subordinates, and others who are knowledgeable about their behavior.

Four questions need to be answered: Who is best qualified? Who is most reliable? Who is most available? Are there any reasons why one or more of the possible candidates should not be used?

If we try to determine who is best qualified, the answer is probably the subordinates who see the behavior of the trainee on a regular basis. In some cases, others who are neither boss nor subordinate have regular contact with the trainee. And, of course, the trainee knows (or should know) his or her own behavior. Therefore, of the four candidates just named, the immediate supervisor may be the person least qualified to evaluate the trainee unless he or she spends a great deal of time with the trainee.

Who is the most reliable? The trainee may not admit that behavior has not changed. Subordinates can be biased in favor of or against the trainee and therefore give a distorted picture. In fact, anyone can give a distorted picture, depending on his or her attitude toward the trainee or the program. This is why more than one source should be used.

Who is the most available? The answer depends on the particular situation. If interviews are to be conducted, then availability is critical. If a survey questionnaire is used, it is not important. In this case, the answer depends on who is willing to spend the time needed to complete the survey.

Are there any reasons why one or more of the possible candidates should not be used? The answer is yes. For example, asking subordinates for information on the behavior of their supervisor may not set well with the supervisor. However, if the trainee is willing to have subordinates questioned, this may be the best approach of all.

A significant decision is whether to use a questionnaire or an interview. Both have their advantages and disadvantages. The interview gives you an opportunity to get more information. The best approach is to use a patterned interview in which all interviewees are asked the same questions. Then you can tabulate the responses and gather quantitative data on behavior change.

But interviews are very time–consuming, and only a few can be conducted if the availability of the person doing the interviewing is limited. Therefore, a small sample of those trained can be interviewed. However, the sample may not be representative of the behavior change that took place in trainees. And you cannot draw conclusions about the overall change in behavior. Exhibit 6.1 shows a patterned interview that can be used as is or adapted to your particular situation.

A survey questionnaire is usually more practical. If it is designed properly, it can provide the data that you need to evaluate change in behavior. The usual problem of getting people to take the time to complete it is always present. However, you can overcome this problem by motivating the people whom you ask to complete the survey. Perhaps there can be some reward, either intrinsic or extrinsic, for doing it. Or a person can be motivated to do

Exhibit 6.1. Patterned Interview

The interviewer reviews the program with the interviewee and highlights the behaviors that the program encouraged. The interviewer then clarifies the purpose of the interview, which is to evaluate the effectiveness of the course so that improvements can be made in the future. Specifically, the interview will determine the extent to which the suggested behaviors have been applied on the job. If they have not been applied, the interview will seek to learn why not. The interviewer makes it clear that all information will be held confidential so that the answers given can be frank and honest.

1. What specific behaviors were you taught and encouraged to use?

2. When you left the program, how anxious were you to change your behavior on the job?

3. How well-equipped were you to do what was suggested?

4. If you are not doing some of the things that you were encouraged and taught to do, why not?

	How Significant?		
	Very	*To some extent*	*Not*
a. It wasn't practical for my situation.			
b. My boss discourages me from changing.			
c. I haven't found the time.			
d. I tried it, and it didn't work.			
e. Other reasons.			

5. To what extent do you plan to do things differently in the future?

6. What suggestions do you have for making the program more helpful?

---

it as a favor to the person doing the research. Producing information for top management as the reason for doing it may convince some. If the instructor, the person doing the evaluation, or both have built a rapport with those who are asked to complete the survey, they usually will cooperate. Exhibit 6.2 shows a survey questionnaire that you can use as is or adapt to your organization.

Get 100 Percent Response or a Sampling

The dictum that something beats nothing can apply when you evaluate change in behavior. The person doing the evaluation can pick out a few "typical" trainees at random and interview or survey them. Or you can interview or survey the persons most likely not to change. The conclusion might be that, if Joe and Charlie have changed their behavior, then everyone has. This conclusion may or may not be true, but the approach can be practical. Obviously, the best approach is to measure the behavior change in all trainees. In most cases, this is not practical. Each organization must determine the amount of time and money that it can spend on level 3 evaluation and proceed accordingly.

Repeat the Evaluation at Appropriate Times

Some trainees may change their behavior as soon as they return to their job. Others may wait six months or a year or never change. And those who change immediately may revert to the old behavior after trying out the new behavior for a period of time. Therefore, it is important to repeat the evaluation at an appropriate time.

I wish I could describe what an appropriate time is. Each organization has to make the decision on its own, depending on the kind of behavior, the job climate, and other significant factors unique to the situation. I would suggest waiting two or three months before conducting the first evaluation, the exact number depending on the opportunity that trainees have to use the new behavior. Perhaps another six months should elapse before the

Exhibit 6.2. Survey Questionnaire

Instructions: The purpose of this questionnaire is to determine the extent to which those who attended the recent program on leadership methods have applied the principles and techniques that they learned there to the job. The results of the survey will help us to assess the effectiveness of the program and identify ways in which it can be made more practical for those who attend. Please be frank and honest in your answers. Your name is strictly optional. The only reason we ask is that we might want to follow up on your answers to get more comments and suggestions from you.

Please circle the appropriate response after each question.

5 = Much more   4 = Some more   3 = The same   2 = Some less   1 = Much less

Understanding and Motivating	*Time and energy spent after the program compared to time and energy spent before the program*				
1. Getting to know my employees	5	4	3	2	1
2. Listening to my subordinates	5	4	3	2	1
3. Praising good work	5	4	3	2	1
4. Talking with employees about their families and other personal interests	5	4	3	2	1
5. Asking subordinates for their ideas	5	4	3	2	1
6. Managing by walking around	5	4	3	2	1

Orienting and Training

7. Asking new employees about their families, past experience, etc.	5	4	3	2	1
8. Taking new employees on a tour of the department and other facilities	5	4	3	2	1
9. Introducing new employees to their coworkers	5	4	3	2	1
10. Using the four-step method when training new and present employees	5	4	3	2	1
11. Being patient when employees don't learn as fast as I think they should	5	4	3	2	1
12. Tactfully correcting mistakes and making suggestions	5	4	3	2	1
13. Using the training inventory and timetable concept	5	4	3	2	1

What would have made the program more practical and helpful to you?

Name (optional) _____

evaluation is repeated. And, depending on circumstances and the time available, a third evaluation could be made three to six months later.

Consider Cost Versus Benefits

Just as with other investments, you should compare the cost of evaluating change in behavior with the benefits that could result from the evaluation. In many organizations, much of the cost of evaluation at level 3 is in the staff time that it takes to do. And time is money. Other costs of evaluation can include the hiring of an outside expert to guide or even conduct the evaluation. For example, I have been hired by Kemper Insurance, TRW, Hershey, State Farm Insurance, and AT&T to present and discuss the four levels of evaluation with their training staff. At Kemper, I was asked to offer specific suggestions and return three months later to comment on the evaluations that they had done. (Chapter 10 describes one of their evaluations.) In these instances, I was called in not to evaluate a specific program but to provide guidelines and specific suggestions on how programs could be evaluated at all four levels. Other consultants can be called in to evaluate the changes in behavior that result from a specific program. You should consider such costs as these when you decide whether to evaluate changes in behavior.

The other factor to consider is the benefits that can be derived from evaluation including changes in behavior and final results. The greater the potential benefits, the more time and money can be spent on the evaluation not only of behavior change but in level 4 also. Another important consideration is the number of times the program will be offered. If it is run only once and it will not be repeated, there is little justification for spending time and money to evaluate possible changes in behavior. However, if a program is going to be repeated, the time and money spent evaluating it can be justified by the possible improvements in future programs.

It is important to understand that change in behavior is not an end in itself. Rather, it is a means to an end: the final results that can be achieved if change in behavior occurs. If no change in behavior occurs, then no improved results can occur. At the same time, even if change in behavior does occur, positive results may not be achieved. A good example is the principle and technique of managing by walking around (MBWA). Some organizations, including United Airlines and Hewlett-Packard, have found that higher morale and increased productivity can result. These organizations therefore encourage managers at all levels to walk among the lowest-level employees to show that they care. Picture a manager who has never shown concern for people. He attends a seminar at which he is told to change his behavior by walking around among lower-level employees to show that he cares. So the manager — for the first time — changes his behavior. He asks one employee about the kids. He comments to another employee regarding a vacation trip that the employee's family is planning. And he asks another employee about Sam, the pet dog. (The manager has learned about these things before talking to the three employees.) What are the chances that the three employees are now going to be motivated to increase their productivity because the manager really cares? Or will they look with suspicion on the new behavior and wonder what the boss is up to? The manager's change in behavior could even have negative results. This possibility underlines the fact that some behavior encouraged in the classroom is not appropriate for all participants. Encouraging supervisors to empower employees is a behavior that would not be appropriate in departments that had a lot of new employees, employees with negative attitudes, or employees with limited knowledge.

Summary

Level 3 evaluation determines the extent to which change in behavior occurs because of the training program. No final results can be expected unless a positive change in behavior occurs. Therefore, it is important to see whether the knowledge, skills, and/or attitudes learned in the program transfer to the job. The process of evaluating is complicated and often difficult to do. You have to decide whether to use interviews, survey questionnaires, or both. You must also decide whom to contact for the evaluation.

Two other difficult decisions are when and how often to conduct the evaluation. Whether to use a control group is still another important consideration. The sum of these factors discourages most trainers from even making an attempt to evaluate at level 3. But something beats nothing, and I encourage trainers to do some evaluating of behavior even if it isn't elaborate or scientific. Simply ask a few people, Are you doing anything different on the job because you attended the training program?

If the answer is yes, ask, Can you briefly describe what you are doing and how it is working out? If you are not doing anything different, can you tell me why? Is it because you didn't learn anything that you can use on the job? Does your boss encourage you to try out new things, or does your boss discourage any change in your behavior? Do you plan to change some of your behavior in the future? If the answer is yes, ask, What do you plan to do differently?

Questions like these can be asked on a questionnaire or in an interview. A tabulation of the responses can provide a good indication of changes in behavior.

If the program is going to be offered a number of times in the future and the potential results of behavior changes are significant, then a more systematic and extensive approach should be used. The guidelines in this chapter will prove helpful.

Chapter 7

Evaluating Results

Now comes the most important and difficult of all — determining what final results occurred because of attendance and participation in a training program. Trainers ask questions like these:

How much did quality improve because of the training program on total quality improvement that we have presented to all supervisors and managers, and how much has it contributed to profits?

How much did productivity increase because we conducted a program on diversity in the workforce for all supervisors and managers?

What reduction did we get in turnover and scrap rate because we taught our foremen and supervisors to orient and train new employees?

How much has management by walking around improved the quality of work life?

What has been the result of all our programs on interpersonal communications and human relations?

How much has productivity increased and how much have costs reduced because we have trained our employees to work in self-directed work teams?

What tangible benefits have we received for all the money we have spent on programs on leadership, time management, and decision making?

How much have sales increased as the result of teaching our salespeople such things as market research, overcoming objections, and closing a sale?

What is the return on investment for all the money we spend on training?

All these and many more questions usually remain unanswered for two reasons: First, trainers don't know how to measure the results and compare them with the cost of the program. Second, even if they do know how, the findings probably provide evidence at best and not clear proof that the positive results come from the training program. There are exceptions, of course. Increases in sales may be found to be directly related to a sales training program, and a program aimed specifically at reducing accidents or improving quality can be evaluated to show direct results from the training program.

A number of years ago, Jack Jenness, a friend of mine at Consolidated Edison in New York, was asked by his boss to show results in terms of dollars and cents from an expensive program on leadership that they were giving to middle- and upper-level managers. The company had hired consultants from St. Louis at a very high fee to conduct the program. I told Jack, "There is no way it can be done!" He said, "That's what I told my boss." Jack then asked me to come out to his organization to do two things: Conduct a workshop with their trainers on the four levels of evaluation, and tell his boss that it couldn't be done. I did the first. I didn't get a chance to do the second because the boss had either been convinced and didn't see the need, or he didn't have the time or desire to hear what I had to say.

This example is unusual at this point in history, but it might not be too unusual in the future. Whenever I get together with trainers, I ask, "How much pressure are you getting from top management to prove the value of your training programs in results, such as dollars and cents?" Only a few times have they said they were feeling such pressure. But many trainers have told me that the day isn't too far off when they expect to be asked to provide such proof.

When we look at the objectives of training programs, we find that almost all aim at accomplishing some worthy result. Often, it is improved quality, productivity, or safety. In other programs, the objective is improved morale or better teamwork, which, it is hoped, will lead to better quality, productivity, safety, and profits. Therefore, trainers look at the desired end result and say to themselves and others, "What behavior on the part of supervisors and managers will achieve these results?" Then they decide what knowledge, skills, and attitudes supervisors need in order to behave in that way. Finally, they determine the training needs and proceed to do the things described in Chapter 1. In so doing, they hope (and sometimes pray) that the trainees will like the program; learn the knowledge, skills, and attitudes taught; and transfer them to the job. The first three levels of evaluation attempt to determine the degree to which these three things have been accomplished.

So now we have arrived at the final level, What final results were accomplished because of the training program? Here are some guidelines that will be helpful:

Guidelines for Evaluating Results

1. Use a control group if practical.
2. Allow time for results to be achieved.
3. Measure both before and after the program if practical.
4. Repeat the measurement at appropriate times.
5. Consider cost versus benefits.
6. Be satisfied with evidence if proof is not possible.

Do these guidelines look familiar? They are almost the same ones that were listed in Chapter 6 for evaluating change in behavior. Some have the same principles and difficulty. At least one (number 3) is much easier.

Use a Control Group If Practical

Enough has been said about control groups in Chapters 5 and 6 that I do not need to dwell on it here. The reason for control groups is always the same: to eliminate the factors other than training that could have caused the changes observed to take place.

In a sales training program, for example, it might be quite easy to control groups. If salespeople in different parts of the country are selling the same products, then a new sales training program can be conducted in some areas and not in others. By measuring the sales figures at various times after the program and comparing them with sales before the program, you can readily see differences. The increase (or decrease) in sales in the regions where the new sales program has been presented can easily be compared to the increase (or decrease) in areas where the program has not been presented. This does not prove that the difference resulted from the training program, even if the control and experimental groups were equal. Other factors may have influenced the sales. These factors can include such things as these: a new competitor has entered the marketplace, a good customer has gone out of business, the economy in a region has gone bad, a competitor has gone out of business, a new customer has moved into the region, or a present customer got a new order that requires your product. These and other factors force us to use the term *evidence* in place of *proof.* (See Chapter 18.)

Allow Time for Results to Be Achieved

In the sales example just cited, time has to elapse before the evaluation can be done. How long does it take for a customer to increase orders? There is no sure answer to the question because each situation is different. Likewise, if a program aims to teach such subjects as leadership, communication, motivation, and team building, the time between training and application on the job may be different for each individual. And improved results, if they occur, will lag behind the changes in behavior. In deciding on the time lapse before evaluating, a trainer must consider all the factors that are involved.

Measure Both Before and
After the Program If Practical

This is easier to do when you are evaluating results than when you are evaluating changes in behavior. Records are usually available to determine the situation before the program. If a program aims at reducing the frequency and severity of accidents, figures are readily available. Figures are also available for the sales example just used. The same is true for quality, production, turnover, number of grievances, and absenteeism. For morale and attitudes, preprogram figures may also be available from attitude surveys and performance appraisal forms.

Repeat the Measurement at Appropriate Times

Each organization must decide how often and when to evaluate. Results can change at any time in either a positive or negative direction. It is up to the training professional to determine the influence of training on these results. For example, sales may have increased because of a big push and close supervision to use a new technique. When the push is over and the boss has other things to do, the salesperson may go back to the old way, and negative results may occur.

Consider Cost Versus Benefits

How much does it cost to evaluate at this level? Generally, it isn't nearly as costly as it is to evaluate change in behavior. The figures you need are usually available. The difficulty is to determine just what figures are meaningful and to what extent they are related, directly or otherwise, to the training. I almost laugh when I hear people say that training professionals should be able to show benefits in terms of return on investment (ROI). The same thought occurs to me when they expect trainers to relate training programs directly to profits. Just think of all the factors that affect profits. And you can add to the list when you consider all the things that affect ROI.

The amount of money that should be spent on level 4 evaluation should be determined by the amount of money that the training program costs, the potential results that can accrue because of the program, and the number of times that the program will be offered. The higher the value of potential results and the more times the program will be offered, the more time and money should be spent. The value of the actual results (if it can be determined accurately) should then be compared to the cost of the program. The results of this evaluation should determine whether the program should be continued.

Be Satisfied with Evidence If Proof Is Not Possible

In a court of law, juries are asked to determine if the defendant is guilty beyond a reasonable doubt. The fact that some people don't tell the truth and that testimony and "facts" can conflict necessitates this concept instead of the concept of proof.

The situation is similar when we evaluate results. We look for evidence beyond a reasonable doubt that the results observed occurred because of a training program. Some critics can say, "Isn't it possible that other factors could have influenced the results?" The answer is usually yes.

For example, turnover in a certain company was far too high. The main reason for the turnover, as determined by the training department, was that supervisors and foremen were doing a poor job of orienting and training new employees. Therefore, a training program on how to orient and train employees was conducted in April for all supervisors and foremen. Here are the turnover figures before and after the April training.

Oct.	Nov.	Dec.	Jan.	Feb.	Mar.	**Apr.**	May	June	July	Aug.	Sept.
6%	7%	5%	7%	6%	7%	6%	4%	2%	2%	2%	3%

It seems obvious that the training program caused the positive results. After all, the objective of the training program was to reduce turnover, and turnover certainly dropped. But some wise guy asks, "Are you sure that some other factor didn't cause the reduction?" And the trainer says, "Like what?" And the wise guy says, "The unemployment figure in your city went way up, and new employees got a nice raise, and the figures for last year were about the same, and I understand that your employment department is hiring more mature people instead of kids right out of high school." And so we have to be satisfied with evidence instead of proof. This is really not bad, because most upper-level managers will be happy with evidence, because until this time all they have heard about training has been the reactions of those who attended.

Summary

Evaluating results, level 4, provides the greatest challenge to training professionals. After all, that is why we train, and we ought to be able to show tangible results that more than pay for the cost of the training. In some cases, such evaluation can be done and quite easily. Programs that aim at increasing sales, reducing accidents, reducing turnover, and reducing scrap rates can often be evaluated in terms of results. And the cost of the program isn't too difficult to determine. A comparison can readily show that training pays off.

Most of the programs that I teach have results in mind. When I conduct a management workshop on how to manage change, I certainly hope that those who attend will make better changes in the future and that the changes will be accepted and implemented enthusiastically. The results will be such things as better quality of work, more productivity, more job satisfaction, and fewer mistakes. When I teach how to improve communication effectiveness, I expect participating supervisors to communicate better on the job afterwards and the result to be fewer misunderstandings, fewer mistakes, improved rapport between supervisor and subordinate, and other positive results. When I teach leadership, motivation, and decision making, I expect participants to understand what I teach, accept my ideas, and use them on the job. This will, of course, end up with tangible results. But how can I tell? Can I prove or even find evidence beyond a reasonable doubt that the final results occur? The answer is a resounding no. There are too many other factors that affect results.

So what should a trainer do when top management asks for tangible evidence that training programs are paying off? Sometimes, you can find evidence that positive results have occurred. In other situations, you will have to go back a level or two and evaluate changes in behavior, learning, or both. In many cases, positive reaction sheets from supervisors and managers will convince top management. After all, if top management has any confidence in the management team, isn't it enough to know that the supervisors and managers feel the training is worthwhile?

A final word: If your programs aim at tangible results rather than teach management concepts, theories, and principles, then it is desirable to evaluate in terms of results. Consider the guidelines given in this chapter. And most important, be satisfied with evidence, because proof is usually impossible to get.

Chapter 8

Implementing the Four Levels

Everybody talks about it, but nobody does anything about it. When Mark Twain said this, he was talking about the weather. It also applies to evaluation—well, almost. My contacts with training professionals indicate that most use some form of reaction, "smile," or "happiness" sheets. Some of these sheets are, in my opinion, very good and provide helpful information that measures customer satisfaction. Others do not meet the guidelines that I listed in Chapter 4. And many trainers ignore critical comments by saying, "Well, you can't please everybody" or "I know who said that, and I am not surprised."

Where do I start? What do I do first? These are typical questions from trainers who are convinced that evaluation is important but have done little about it.

My suggestion is to start at level 1 and proceed through the other levels as time and opportunity allow. Some trainers are anxious to get to level 3 or 4 right away because they think the first two aren't as important. Don't do it. Suppose, for example, that you evaluate at level 3 and discover that little or no change in behavior has occurred. What conclusions can you draw? The first conclusion is probably that the training program was no good, and we had better discontinue it or at least modify it. This conclusion may be entirely wrong. As I described in Chapter 3, the reason for no change in job behavior may be that the climate prevents it. Supervisors may have gone back to the job with the necessary knowledge, skills, and attitudes, but the boss wouldn't allow change to take place. Therefore, it is important to evaluate at level 2 so you can determine whether the reason for no change in behavior was lack of learning or negative job climate.

The first step for you to take in implementing the evaluation concepts, theories, and techniques described in the preceding chapters is to understand the guidelines of level 1 and apply them in every program. Use a philosophy that states, "If my customers are unhappy, it is my fault, and my challenge is to please them." If you don't, your entire training program is in trouble. It is probably true that you seldom please everyone. For example, it is a rare occasion when everyone in my training classes grades me excellent. Nearly always some participants are critical of my sense of humor, some content that I presented, or the quality of the audiovisual aids. I often find myself justifying what I did and ignoring their comments, but I shouldn't do that. My style of humor, for example, is to embarrass participants, I hope in a pleasant way so that they don't resent it. That happens to be my style, and most people enjoy and appreciate it. If I get only one critical comment from a group of twenty-five, I will ignore it and continue as I did in the past. However, if the reaction is fairly common because I have overdone it, then I will take the comment seriously and change my approach.

I used to tell a funny story in class. It was neither dirty nor ethnic. Nearly everyone else thought it was funny, too, and I had heard no objections to it. One day, I conducted a training class with social workers. I told the story at the beginning of the class and proceeded to do the training. After forty minutes, I asked whether anyone had a comment or question. One lady raised her hand and said, "I was offended by the joke you told at the beginning of the session, and I didn't listen to anything you said after that!"

I couldn't believe it. I was sure she was the only one who felt that way, so I asked the question, "Did any others feel the same way?" Seven other women raised their hands. There were about forty-five people in the class, so the percentage was very much in my favor. But I decided that that particular joke had no place in future meetings. If she had been the only one, I probably would still be telling it.

The point is this: Look over all the reaction sheets, and read the comments. Consider each one. Is there a suggestion that will improve future programs? If yes, use it. If it is an isolated comment that will not improve future programs, appreciate it, but ignore it.

Evaluating at level 2 isn't that difficult. All you need to do is to decide what knowledge, skills, and attitudes you want participants to have at the end of the program. If there is a possibility that one or more of these three things already exist, then a pretest is necessary. If you are presenting something entirely new, then no pretest is necessary. You can use a standardized test if you can find one that covers the things you are teaching. Several examples were given in Chapter 5. Or you can develop your own test to cover the knowledge and attitudes that you are teaching. An example from MGIC was also given in Chapter 5. Study the guidelines and suggestions from Chapter 5, and then do it!

Levels 3 and 4 are not easy. A lot of time will be required to decide on an evaluation design. A knowledge of statistics to determine the level of significance may be desirable. Check with the research people in your organization for help in the design. If necessary, you may have to call in an outside consultant to help you or even do the evaluation for you. Remember the principle that the possible benefits from an evaluation should exceed the cost of doing the evaluation, and be satisfied with evidence if proof is not possible.

There is another important principle that applies to all four levels: You can borrow evaluation forms, designs, and procedures from others, but you cannot borrow evaluation results. If another organization offers the same program as you do and they evaluate it, you can borrow their evaluation methods and procedures, but you can't say, "They evaluated it and found these results. Therefore, we don't have to do it, because we know the results we would get."

Learn all you can about evaluation. Find out what others have done. Look for forms, methods, techniques, and designs that you can copy or adapt. Ignore the results of these other evaluations, except out of curiosity.

And now for some specific suggestions.

1. Study the case studies in Part Two of this book. They illustrate all four levels.

2. Study one or both of the following manuals from the American Society for Training and Development (ASTD; 1640 King Street, Alexandria, VA 22313–2043; 703/683–8100):

Kirkpatrick, Donald. *Evaluating Training Programs.* (This manual contains all the articles on evaluation that appeared in ASTD's *Training and Development* between 1965 and 1975.)

Kirkpatrick, Donald. *More Evaluating Training Programs.* (This manual contains all the articles on evaluation that appeared in ASTD's *Training and Development* between 1976 and 1986.)

3. Read one or more of the following books:

Basarab, David J., Sr., and Root, Darrell K. *The Training Evaluation Process.* Norwell, Mass.: Kluwer, 1992.

Brinkerhoff, Robert. *Achieving Results from Training.* San Francisco: Jossey-Bass, 1988.

Holcomb, Jane. *Making Training Worth Every Penny.* Playa del Rey, Calif.: On-Target Training, 1993.

Jackson, Terence. *Evaluation: Relating Training to Business Performance.* San Diego, Calif.: University Associates, 1989.

Kirkpatrick, Donald. *How to Train and Develop Supervisors.* New York: AMACOM, 1993.

Phillips, Jack. *Training Evaluation and Measurement Methods.* (2nd ed.) Houston: Gulf, 1991.

Robinson, Dana, and Robinson, James. *Training for Impact.* San Francisco: Jossey-Bass, 1989.

Zemke, Ron, Standke, Linda, and Jones, Philip (eds.). *Cost-Effective Training and Measuring the Results.* Minneapolis: *Training Magazine,* 1981. (This is a collection of many short articles by different authors on various aspects of training, including evaluation.)

4. If advisable and cost-effective, hire a qualified consultant to help you with your evaluation.

In teaching management courses, I usually start by telling the group about a study made by the Society for Advancement of Management, a branch of the American Management Association. A special task force was assigned the job of deciding on a definition of management. The task force decided that management is a science and an art. It defined these two words as follows: "As a science, it is organized knowledge—concepts, theory, principles, and techniques. As an art, it is the application of the organized knowledge to realities in a situation, usually with blend or compromise, to obtain desired practical results."

I would like to use the same definition for *evaluation*. It is a science and an art. This book provides the organized knowledge—concepts, theory, principles, and techniques. It is up to you to do the application. May you be successful in doing it.

PART TWO

CASE STUDIES OF IMPLEMENTATION

In order to make this book as practical and helpful as possible, I invited a number of training professionals to describe an evaluation that they had done in implementing one or more of the four levels. I looked for variety in terms of the type of program as well as the type of organization in which the evaluation had been done. I also wanted case studies of evaluations that ranged from the simple to the complex. The case studies from Motorola, Arthur Andersen, and Intel were written by evaluation specialists. All three organizations have a separate department to evaluate programs.

All the case studies were written especially for this book with the exception of Chapters 14, 19, 20, and 21. These chapters reprint articles that appeared in *Training and Development,* a publication of the American Society for Training and Development.

When you study these cases, it is important to understand that you can borrow forms, designs, and techniques and adapt them to your own organization. This may save you a lot of time and frustration when making decisions on what to evaluate and how to do it. If you want more details on the evaluations, I am sure that the authors will be happy to oblige.

Chapter 9

Evaluating a Training Program for Nonexempt Employees

This case study is an example of a relatively simple approach for evaluating at all four levels. It includes a reaction sheet and a survey form that can be tabulated on a computer. The evaluation of results compared turnover figures for those trained with figures on those who were not trained. These figures were then converted into dollar savings. The design of the evaluation is readily adaptable to other organizations.

First Union National Bank

Patrick O'Hara, Assistant Vice President
Human Resources Division, Training and Development
First National Bank, Charlotte, North Carolina

CARE

A major goal of First Union is to let employees know how much they and their contribution to the success and growth of First Union are valued. Personal development is one strategy.

CARE I is a program that was developed to provide a developmental opportunity for the nonexempt employees who historically have not been the focus of personal development training. As the corporation has expanded over the last several years, there has been tremendous change and upheaval. During mergers and consolidations, employees have the pressures that all this change has brought to bear. CARE is a one-day program devoted to the bank's largest population, the nonexempt employees who have shouldered major responsibilities throughout this growth cycle at First Union.

CARE is an acronym for Communication, Awareness, Renewal, and Empowerment. The learning objectives are:

- Increase self-awareness by use of self-assessment tools and group feedback.
- Increase understanding of communication styles and develop flexibility in one's own communication style.
- Increase communication effectiveness by exposure to and practice in assertiveness concepts and skills.
- Understand and implement the steps of goal setting as a tool in career renewal.

Input from employee focus groups was instrumental in developing the course design.

The program is offered on an ongoing basis for new employees. The majority of CARE I training occurred in 1991. More than 10,000 employees have attended CARE I.

Here is a brief description of the CARE program, with an indication of the activities and materials used:

Morning:
- Johari Window
- Self-awareness: DESA instrument explained and processed
- Assertiveness in communication, lecturette, role playing, discussion on using a journal to help increase assertive behavior

Lunch: As a group

Afternoon:
- Assertiveness continued
- Creating your future: goal-setting process as a tool for personal renewal (process explained and exercises processed)

- Personal empowerment: where and how it begins (discussion to tie the day's activities to the overriding theme of empowerment)

Closing Ceremony: Three Gifts

- Gift from corporation: a mustard seed in a lucite cube with the CARE logo
- Gift from each other: positive quotes for other participants sealed in an envelope to be opened in one month
- Gift to self: Have participants write down what they want to give themselves in the coming year (could be a healthier body, etc.), put in sealed envelope, and open in two months

Evaluation Plan

Because this was such a massive effort on the part of the corporation, it was decided that the results should be evaluated. It was decided to start with the four-level Kirkpatrick evaluation model and create several measurement instruments.

1. Participant reactions

Our standard end-of-course evaluation form was modified to fit the CARE program. Because it was a personal development course, the intent was to ask participants how it related to their personal development. The questionnaires were administered at the end of the day by the trainer and collected and returned to the Corporate Training and Development department for processing. Exhibit 9.1 shows the evaluation form.

2. and 3. Learning gains and behavior changes

Again, because CARE was a personal development course, it was felt that both the learning and any resulting changes in behavior were of a very subjective and personal nature. To evaluate on the second and third levels (learning gain and behavior change), the company sent a questionnaire to a random sample of the participants asking them about their learning and changes in their behavior. This instrument was mailed to participants at the end of each quarter, so that the longest period of time between the class and the questionnaire was about ninety days. The

Exhibit 9.1. CARE Evaluation Form, National Computer Systems

Name of Instructor _____

Location _____

Date _____

National Computer Systems

Instructions: When marking each answer:

- Use a No. 2 pencil only.
- Circle appropriate number.
- Cleanly erase any marks you wish to change.

Please use the following scale to record your thoughts about the course content:

1 = *Disagree strongly*
2 = *Disagree*
3 = *Neither agree nor disagree*
4 = *Agree*
5 = *Agree strongly*

Content

1. The skills taught in this class are relevant to my personal development.   1 2 3 4 5

2. This class helped me develop those skills.   1 2 3 4 5

3. The material was clearly organized.   1 2 3 4 5

4. The course content met my needs.   1 2 3 4 5

5. Comments:

Instruction

The course instructor

6. Facilitated class discussions effectively.   1 2 3 4 5

7. Listened carefully to participants.   1 2 3 4 5

8. Assisted in linking concepts to actual interpersonal situations.   1 2 3 4 5

9. Had excellent presentation skills.   1 2 3 4 5

10. Comments:

Overall

11. Rank your overall satisfaction with the program.   1 2 3 4 5

Thank you for taking the time to give constructive feedback on this course. Your responses will be used to improve future courses.

Exhibit 9.2. Insti-Survey, National Computer Systems

Directions: Thank you for taking the time to complete this short survey.

Please use a No. 2 pencil. Cleanly erase any responses you want to change.

Please use the following scale:

A = *Agree strongly*
B = *Agree somewhat*
C = *Neutral*
D = *Disagree somewhat*
E = *Disagree strongly*

Because of my CARE Class, I

1. Am more self-aware.   A   B   C   D   E

2. Am better able to communicate with others.   A   B   C   D   E

3. Am seeking more feedback on strengths and areas to improve.   A   B   C   D   E

4. Feel more personally empowered.   A   B   C   D   E

5. Can better respond to aggressive behavior.   A   B   C   D   E

6. Can better respond to nonassertive behavior.   A   B   C   D   E

7. Am more likely to assert myself now.   A   B   C   D   E

8. Am better able to set goals for myself now.   A   B   C   D   E

9. See how goal setting helps me make some positive changes.   A   B   C   D   E

10. Feel more valued as a First Union Employee now.   A   B   C   D   E

---

completed forms were returned to the Corporate Training and Development Department for processing. Exhibit 9.2 shows the questionnaire.

4. Organizational impact

It was determined that the best way to evaluate the impact on the organization was to look at turnover. The rationale was that, if employees did indeed feel valued by the company, they would be less likely to leave. Turnover is also one of the most reliable bits of information tracked at First Union.

Numbers on turnover were kept not only for employees who had participated in the program but also for those who had not. The employees selected to participate in the CARE program were determined in a fairly random manner, since the intent of the program was that eventually all nonexempt employees would participate. An extra step was taken, and statistics were run on other information kept in our Human Resource database to determine whether we had other information about participants that might be related to turnover. Last, some simple calculations were made to determine what a reduction in turnover might have saved the corporation in real dollars.

Evaluation Results

The results of the evaluations were surprising, to say the least.
 1. Participants' reactions
 Our course evaluation was separated into three categories: content, instruction, and an overall evaluation of the program. We used a five-point scale to scale responses, with 5 being the highest response possible and 1 the lowest. For the CARE program, we consistently received the following scores:

Content   4.45
Instruction 4.76
Overall   4.69

While it is felt that these scores can always be improved, they are high.
 2. and 3. Learning gains and behavior changes
 The responses to the various questions are combined to determine a score for the achievement of the course objectives overall. Once again, a five-point scale was used in which 5 was the best and 1 signalled cause for concern. On this measure, an average of 3.9 was received. Given the fact that time had passed and that learning and behavior changes normally drop off over time, this, too, is a very good score.
 4. Organizational impact
 The results of the level 4 evaluation were probably the most exciting from an organizational perspective. We found that the difference in turnover was 14 percent. Turnover rates for the CARE group were running at about 4.2 percent for the year, while

for the non-CARE group they were 18.2 percent. This finding was extremely exciting.

In addition, we pulled several pieces of data from the corporate Human Resources database on all participants. We checked things like gender, age, and time with the company to see whether some other variable might affect the results. We brought in a consultant to help determine what information might be looked at, and the consultant ran a discriminant analysis on the resulting data for us. Nothing else could be found that seemed to be contributing to the reduction in turnover among the CARE group. This was pretty good evidence that the program was influencing the reduction in turnover.

As the last step in the process, we calculated real dollar savings for the program. To do this, we determined our cost for hiring and training tellers. First Union has a lot of tellers, and we know a lot about their hiring and training costs. Tellers also made up about 33 percent of the CARE participants.

It costs $2,700 to hire and train a teller. It costs $110 to put a teller through CARE. If CARE training saves the company from having to hire and train a teller, we save $2,590. Given the number of tellers put through the CARE program, the estimated savings to the company were over $1,000,000 in 1991, and that was for only one-third of the CARE group. It is expected that the costs of hiring and training for the other two-thirds are the same or higher on average. This means that the corporation saved a lot of money by offering the program to employees. This saving would have more than funded the entire CARE program.

After conducting what is felt to be a fairly rigorous evaluation of the CARE program in a business environment, we know that

- Particpants reacted very favorably to the program.
- Participants feel that they learned and are using new skills.
- More participants than nonparticipants are staying at First Union.
- First Union not only helped employees grow and develop personally but also benefited in a real, quantifiable way.

Chapter 10

Evaluating a Training Course on Performance Appraisal and Coaching

This study is one of the most complete that I have seen. The evaluation covered all four levels. The program evaluated was a pilot program conducted at the Charlotte, North Carolina, branch of the Kemper National Insurance Companies. The evaluation was planned and implemented by the Corporate Education Department in the home office. Of special interest is the summary of results communicated to executives concerned with the program.

Kemper National Insurance Companies

Judith P. Clarke, Training Manager
Corporate Education Department, Long Grove, Illinois

Need and Purpose

Our training program is a success if it accomplishes four objectives: Participants like the program, participants gain needed knowledge and skills, participants apply what they learned to their jobs, and participants assist the company in achieving its mission and objectives. The purpose of the program is to improve performance. The purpose of evaluation is to verify and improve the effectiveness of training. The evaluation design includes ways and means of measuring the effectiveness of the program in achieving each of the four objectives just defined.

The Training Course

The program was conducted at the Charlotte branch of Kemper. All supervisors and managers attended the course during a three-month period between December 1989 and March 1990. The program and its evaluation received the complete support of the branch manager. Exhibit 10.1 describes the program content and objectives.

Evaluation Design

Both quantitative and qualitative data were collected. Data collection techniques included existing tools as well as measurements designed for this evaluation. This section describes the data collection tools that we used for the four levels on which we evaluated the training program.

1. *Reaction:* How well did the participants like the training? Each participant completed the reaction sheet shown in Exhibit 10.2 at the end of the course. The results were tabulated and summarized.

2. *Learning:* What knowledge and skills did participants gain from the program? We collected data by administering the Performance Appraisal Skills Inventory (King of Prussia, Pa.: Organization Design and Development, 1987) before and after training. The inventory contains eighteen performance appraisal situations. For each situation, the participant selects the best answer from four possible choices.

3. *Behavior:* To what extent have participants transferred knowledge and skills learned in the program to their jobs in these four areas: preparing for the performance appraisal, establishing two-way communication with subordinates, gaining agreement on the appraisal, and documenting the report form.

To collect data, we used results from the Performance Appraisal Report Form Checklist shown in Exhibit 10.3, administered

Exhibit 10.1. Performance Appraisal and Coaching Seminar

Objectives

During this course, participants will

1. Self-assess individual strengths and weaknesses in the skill areas necessary to establish two-way communication and gain agreement in the six steps of the performance appraisal discussion:

- Building trust
- Opening
- Accomplishments and concerns
- Planning
- Evaluating and rating
- Closing

2. Identify individual improvement goals for strengthening skills needed for conducting effective performance appraisal discussions.

3. Practice applying the following coaching process to the six steps of the performance appraisal discussion:

- Identify the situation.
- Clarify information.
- Explore options.
- Agree on actions.
- Follow up.

4. Learn to recognize when specific coaching techniques can be used to establish two-way communication and reduce defensiveness during the performance appraisal discussion.

5. Analyze various ways in which both the employee and the supervisor can prepare for the performance appraisal discussion:

- Reviewing objectives, standards, and reports
- Employee self-appraisal
- Input from next-level manager

6. Define each section of the performance appraisal report form and explain how to use it as a tool in the performance appraisal discussion.

7. Explain how the wording of the performance appraisal report form can enhance the clarity of the completed form and reinforce the interactive tone of the overall process.

8. Demonstrate ability in writing

- Performance improvement needs
- Performance improvement objectives
- Achievement of prior objectives

9. Identify the criteria for a timely, high-quality performance appraisal report form through the use of a checklist.

Exhibit 10.2. Reaction Sheet

Course Title: _____

Instructor(s): _____   Date: _____

Your evaluation of this course will assist in making future courses more effective.

A. *Instructions:* Please indicate a rating for each
   statement below by circling a number on the
   scale to the right:

	Strongly agree			*Strongly disagree*

1. Course objectives were clearly stated and easily   5 4 3 2 1
   understood.
   Comments:

2. Course objectives were met.   5 4 3 2 1
   Comments:

3. Course met my personal expectations.   5 4 3 2 1
   Comments:

4. Time allotted for various segments was appropriate.   5 4 3 2 1
   Comments:

	High			*Low*

5. To what degree was the course relevant to your job?   5 4 3 2 1
   Comments:

6. How would you rate your personal interest in this   5 4 3 2 1
   course?
   Comments:

B. To what degree did the following contribute to
   your achieving the course objectives?

7. Printed participant materials (participant guide,   5 4 3 2 1
   handouts, etc.).
   Comments:

8. Audiovisual materials (tapes, videos, overheads, etc.).   5 4 3 2 1
   Comments:

9. Discussion(s) with other participants.   5 4 3 2 1
   Comments:

Exhibit 10.3. Performance Appraisal Report Form Checklist

On the basis of the completed appraisals that you have brought to the course, how would you answer these questions?

Performance Standards   Yes   No

- Do standards reflect the current job?   ☐   ☐
- Are standards attached and evaluated?   ☐   ☐

Attendance

- Are attendance problems documented according to policy?   ☐   ☐
- Have you refrained from describing the personal reasons
  for absences?   ☐   ☐

Achievement of Prior Objectives

- Are prior objectives restated and evaluated?   ☐   ☐
- If prior objectives are not met, are clear circumstances
  or reasons stated?   ☐   ☐
- If prior objectives are not met, will an outside reader
  know how this will affect the performance rating?   ☐   ☐

Attributes

- Are attributes coded properly and supported by job-specific
  behavioral examples?   ☐   ☐
- Are attributes used to recognize and reinforce past
  performance?   ☐   ☐

Performance Improvement Needs: Immediate Needs

- Do the needs relate to failure to meet standards or
  achieve objectives?   ☐   ☐
- Do supporting comments indicate a sense of urgency
  about the need?   ☐   ☐
- Are supporting comments job related and specific?   ☐   ☐
- Do supporting comments reflect input that the
  employee provided about the need?   ☐   ☐

Performance Improvement Needs: Other

- Are the needs specific, and do they involve job-related
  areas that require improvement?   ☐   ☐
- Are they related to the current position?   ☐   ☐
- Do supporting comments reflect input that the employee
  provided about the need?   ☐   ☐

Objectives

- Are performance improvement objectives listed first and
  linked to the need in Section F?   ☐   ☐
- Do they state specifically how well the employee should
  do or achieve?   ☐   ☐

Exhibit 10.3. Performance Appraisal Report Form Checklist *(continued)*

	Yes	No
• Do they state specifically what the employee should do or achieve to be acceptable?	☐	☐
• Do they state specifically under what conditions (time frame, resources, training) the employee should perform?	☐	☐
• Do supporting comments reflect input that the employee provided about the objectives?	☐	☐

Performance Rating

	Yes	No
• Is the rating consistent with the results and narrative of the entire performance analysis?	☐	☐
• Is the rating based on the principle of zero-based appraisal?	☐	☐

Development Objectives (if applicable)

	Yes	No
• Is it clear that development objectives are not used in determining the performance indicator?	☐	☐
• Is it clear that they are not requirements or standards of the current job?	☐	☐
• Are these objectives specific in terms of what the employee should do, how well, and under what conditions?	☐	☐
• Do supporting comments reflect input that the employee provided about the objective?	☐	☐

Promotability

	Yes	No
• Do identified position(s) fit the employee's experience and skills?	☐	☐
• Are listed position(s) properly titled and coded?	☐	☐
• If the employee is immediately promotable to another functional area, has the performance appraisal been signed by another department manager?	☐	☐

Relocation

	Yes	No
• Did you discuss current relocation preferences with the employee at the time of the appraisal?	☐	☐

Supervisor's Comments

	Yes	No
• Are the comments job related and consistent with the rest of the appraisal?	☐	☐
• Does the Comments section effectively summarize the appraisal?	☐	☐

Other

	Yes	No
• Have you completed each section with all the required documentation?	☐	☐
• If the employee is participating in the career development program, is the career development plan properly completed and attached?	☐	☐

Exhibit 10.3. Performance Appraisal Report Form Checklist *(continued)*

	Yes	No
• Does the appraisal reflect evidence of two-way communication?	☐	☐
• Does the appraisal language reflect employee input?	☐	☐
• If a third party reviewed the completed appraisal, would the documentation be clear and consistent throughout each section?	☐	☐
• Is the appraisal free of references to personal issues and circumstances of employee's life?	☐	☐
• Has the appraisal been completed by the due date?	☐	☐

before and after training, the Performance Appraisal Questionnaire for Managers shown in Exhibit 10.4, the Performance Appraisal Questionnaire for Employees shown in Exhibit 10.5, and unobtrusive data, which included informal observations obtained from many sources, including the Human Resources manager, the immediate supervisor of those completing forms and conducting interviews, and those who completed forms and conducted interviews.

4. *Results:* To assess the results, we asked this question: What gain has there been in the achievement of the following two Human Resources objectives? Ninety-five percent of all performance appraisals are completed on schedule, and the quality and accuracy of the appraisals improve in five areas: candidness, completeness, developmental plans, ratings, and feedback.

Data were collected through an analysis by the branch Human Resources manager of completed performance appraisals.

Evaluation Results

The evaluations were conducted as planned, and the results were communicated to executives and other interested and concerned persons as follows:

The performance appraisal and coaching course was designed to improve the skills of managers and supervisors in coaching effectively during the performance appraisal discussion and in writing the performance appraisal report.

Exhibit 10.4. Performance Appraisal Questionnaire for Managers

---

Instructions: This survey is designed to describe your experiences in conducting performance appraisals since completing the performance appraisal and coaching course.

Please answer the questions below by circling the number that corresponds to your response.

1. Characterize your preparation for conducting performance appraisals since completing the course.

	Much easier		Same		More difficult

Preparation is 5 4 3 2 1

Comments:

2. Characterize the actual performance appraisal discussions that you have conducted since completing the course.

	Much easier		Same		More difficult

- Discussing employee strenths 5 4 3 2 1
- Discussing performance problems 5 4 3 2 1
- Overcoming defensiveness 5 4 3 2 1
- Developing an improvement plan 5 4 3 2 1

3. Characterize your documentation of the performance appraisal report form since completing the course.

	Much easier		Same		More difficult

- Documenting performance improvement needs 5 4 3 2 1
- Writing objectives 5 4 3 2 1
- Documenting achievement of prior obejctives 5 4 3 2 1

4. To what degree have you been successful in reaching agreement with your employees on the main issues of the performance appraisal discussion since completing the course?

	High	Medium	Low

    5 4 3 2 1

Comments:

Exhibit 10.4. Performance Appraisal Questionnaire for Managers *(continued)*

---

5. Which aspects of the performance appraisal process are still the most difficult for you? Check your response(s):

_____ Preparing for the performance appraisal

_____ Discussing employee strengths

_____ Discussing performance problems

_____ Developing an improvement plan

_____ Overcoming defensiveness

_____ Conducting the performance appraisal discussion

_____ Reaching agreement on main issues

_____ Documenting performance improvement needs

_____ Writing objectives

_____ Documenting achievement of prior objecives

Please comment on the items that you have checked.

What other comments would you like to make on conducting performance appraisals? (Use the back of this sheet if necessary.)

Please use the enclosed envelope to return the completed questionnaire. Thank you for your cooperation.

The Charlotte branch was selected as the site for piloting the course and for evaluating its effectiveness. The training received the enthusiastic support of the branch manager, Jim Murphy, and of the branch Human Resources manager, Peggy Jones, and it was positively received by the Charlotte supervisors and managers. Forty-one branch supervisors and managers completed the course between December and March, a fact that made it possible to study the effectiveness of training with an entire management staff.

Exhibit 10.5. Performance Appraisal Questionnaire for Employees

---

Instructions: Your manager recently completed a course on performance appraisal. In order to better understand the effectiveness of this course, we are interested in your reactions to your most recent performance appraisal.

Since this questionnaire is anonymous, do *not* sign your name.

Please answer the questions below by circling your response or the number that corresponds to your response.

1. Has your most recent performance appraisal occurred within the last six months?   Yes   No

2. Were you asked to prepare for the performance appraisal discussion?   Yes   No

   If yes, please explain what you did to prepare.

3. During the performance appraisal discussion, what percentage of time did you spend talking?   _____ %

   Comments:

4. Overall, how would you rate your degree of involvement in your most recent performance appraisal discussion?

   High   Medium   Low
   5   4   3   2   1

   Comments:

5. To what degree did your manager listen to your input during the performance appraisal discussion?

   High   Medium   Low
   5   4   3   2   1

   Comments:

6. To what degree did your manager consider your ideas to be important during the performance appraisal discussion?

   High   Medium   Low
   5   4   3   2   1

   Comments:

7. To what degree were you and your manager successful in reaching agreement on the main issues of the performance appraisal discussion?

   High   Medium   Low
   5   4   3   2   1

   Comments:

Please use the enclosed envelope to return the completed questionnaire. Thank you for your cooperation.

Procedure and Findings

Evaluation that verifies and improves the effectiveness of training is conducted at four levels: reaction, learning, behavior, and results. Evidence to determine the effectiveness of training must be gathered at each level. These are the questions that need to be answered at each level of evaluation and the data collection tools that were used in answering each question:

	Evaluation Question	*Data Collection Tool*
Reaction	How did the participants react to the training?	Course reaction sheets
Learning	What information and skills were gained?	Performance appraisal checklist administered before and after training
Behavior	How have participants transferred knowledge and skills to their jobs?	Performance appraisal checklist administered before and after training Manager and employee questionnaires Anecdotal data
Results	What effect has training had on the organization and achievement of its objectives? (Timeliness and quality in performance appraisals are a corporate goal.)	Performance appraisal checklist

The findings at each level of evaluation indicate that the performance appraisal and coaching course makes a difference in increasing both the quality of the coaching that takes place during the discussion and the quality of the performance appraisal report.

Reaction

Level 1 findings indicate that course participants were satisfied customers. The course evaluations received confirmed that participants reacted positively to the course. Positive reactions increase participants' receptivity to the knowledge and skills presented in the course. The majority of participants felt that the course objectives had been met and that the course was highly relevant to their jobs. The average overall rating on a five-point scale was 4.37.

Learning

Level 2 findings indicate that course participants made gains in the knowledge and skills needed to conduct and document quality performance appraisals. Data gathered from administration of the quality checklist before and after training indicate that 94 percent of the performance appraisals written by participants after the course were of higher quality than the appraisals that they had written before training. It was also significant that, while appraisal quality was as low as 54 percent before training, the lowest quality observed after training was 78 percent.

Behavior

Level 3 findings provide evidence that course participants applied the knowledge and skills acquired in the course when they conducted subsequent performance appraisals. Data gathered with the quality checklist before and after training highlighted three areas of particular improvement: two-way discussion, documentation of attributes, and objectives. The course provides practice sessions to enhance skills needed to involve employees in the performance appraisal discussion and to show evidence of discussion and employee input in the performance appraisal report. Appraisals conducted after participation in the course showed nearly four times more two-way discussion after the course than before it.

Performance appraisals are audited by branch Human Resources staff to identify errors and potential problems. When errors are found, a performance appraisal is returned to the appraising supervisor for improvement. Strong evidence that participants applied knowledge and skills learned in the course on the job was provided by an immediate decline in the number of returns. Before the training program, eight appraisals were returned for improvement in one month. After the program, no more than two appraisals per month were returned.

The Charlotte branch Human Resources manager reported that, from the conclusion of the study through the fourth quarter, the number of appraisals returned through the audit had remained low in comparison to previous years. Her report shows the percentage of audited appraisals that were of acceptable quality each quarter after the program.

Q3	90%
Q4	96
Q1	95
Q2	80
Q3	95
Q4	96

The lower quality of appraisals during the second quarter of the second year reflects the fact that five appraisals were returned for clarification of objectives and documentation of the achievement of prior objectives and that one appraisal lacked proper documentation of attendance. The Charlotte branch Human Resources manager is continuing to coach the management staff in these areas, but she states that the narratives now indicate much more two-way discussion than she saw before the training took place.

Another indication that participants applied new knowledge and skills was the results of two questionnaires. One questionnaire was designed for management staff who were trained and the other for the employees who reported to them.

The manager questionnaire showed that 77 percent of the management staff considered handling performance problems within the performance appraisal to be easier after taking the course. Because the skills needed to coach employees with performance improvement needs effectively are practiced during the course, supervisors and managers are likely to find handling performance problems easier because they are more skilled at doing so.

The employee questionnaire was designed to determine how the employees who had been appraised by the trained supervisors felt about how they had been coached. Evidence provided by employees indicated that supervisors were effective in three important areas: employees felt that supervisors listened (83 percent), that supervisors valued their input highly (75 percent), and that agreement was reached on main issues of the performance appraisal (77 percent).

Anecdotal data provided by the Human Resources manager and the participants themselves confirmed that the course had made a difference in the quality of the performance appraisals being written. By the end of the first quarter after the program, the Human Resources manager stated that she was seeing a marked difference in the overall quality of performance appraisals. Participants commented that it was much easier to do the appraisal after they had completed the course.

Results

Level 4 findings were drawn from data collected with the quality checklist before and after training. The course increased the quality of performance appraisals in several important areas: objectives, performance feedback, and completeness. Specific objectives that met the quality criteria presented in the course increased by 36 percent after training.

Performance feedback, both in recognizing employee strengths and in coaching for performance improvement, was of higher quality after the course. The number of appraisals containing attributes supported by behavioral examples of how the employee exhibited the attribute on the job increased by 49 percent.

Additional evidence of effective feedback on performance improvement needs was provided by the 36 percent increase found in specific objectives, which clearly state what the employee will do to maintain or improve performance and how measurement will take place. The language used to document objectives indicates that employees are becoming more involved in discussing and finding solutions to performance issues. Data from the checklist after training showed a 35 percent increase in evidence of discussion.

Conclusions and Recommendations

The evidence presented in this report supports the assumption that the performance appraisal and coaching course results in supervisors and managers who are more confident and competent in conducting quality performance appraisals. The evidence also shows an increase in the number of performance appraisal reports documented correctly.

Skills and knowledge gained during training need to be reinforced on the job. Reinforcement is achieved when all staff are trained with support from top management. Managers who have themselves been trained can coach the supervisors who report to them. Human resources staff can also provide ongoing coaching.

Training all supervisors and managers in one location creates a great opportunity for affecting the culture in terms of the overall desired outcome of the course. The evaluation clearly shows that supervisors now use a joint problem-solving approach to encourage employees to assume responsibility for their own performance. It also shows that supervisors provide candid feedback on all aspects of performance. Managers and supervisors who are more comfortable with the authoritarian management style may find this approach uncomfortable, but when it is modeled and reinforced by their own manager and peers, change is likely to occur.

Chapter 11

Implementing the Kirkpatrick Model as an Up-front Analysis and Evaluation Tool

This unique case study uses the Kirkpatrick four-level model not only as an evaluation tool after the program but also before the program to determine initial training needs and to design the program. For front-end analysis, the instructional designers began with level 4, results, and worked backwards. The program described in this case study was planned and implemented for senior executives at Intel Corporation.

Intel Corporation

Eric Freitag, Training, Evaluation, and Improvement Manager
Intel University, Chandler, Arizona

Introduction

Seven years ago, a group of senior training managers at Intel Corporation determined that they needed a common methodology for evaluating the training that they were conducting. Up to that point, training evaluation had been sporadic. An extensive literature review made it clear that the Kirkpatrick model would provide an effective framework to help drive evaluation across the forty-odd training groups at Intel.

Initial efforts focused on communicating and teaching the Kirkpatrick model to training employees and management. An evaluation of this early implementation of the Kirkpatrick model indicated that training groups had increased the development of level 1–4 evaluations. However, training managers also found that developers did not use a significant amount of the data being gathered for improvement.

On the basis of the early implementation findings, training managers determined that the Kirkpatrick model should be positioned not only at the end of the instructional systems development process but also at the very beginning of the process and that it should be used there in determining the need for training and the design of training. Positioning the model as a front-end analysis tool increased utilization of the data. Project designs included evaluation plans and baselines.

For front-end analysis, the Kirkpatrick model is turned around, and instructional designers begin by asking level 4 questions. Level 4 questions include, What are the business indicators needing improvement? Level 3 questions ask, What changes of behaviors are you expecting to see on the job? Level 2 questions include What is the most appropriate design to increase acquisition and transfer of the required skills and knowledge. And level 1 questions ask, What is the most appropriate intervention design to ensure that participants will be motivated and satisfied? The answers to these questions establish the most appropriate intervention and provide baseline data that can be used to determine training success during the evaluation phase.

Applying the Kirkpatrick Model

Intel's senior management training program applied the Kirkpatrick model as both an analysis and an evaluation tool. One part of the overall program includes senior executives as the target population. The training for senior managers is three days. It has three areas of content: systems thinking in the learning organization, managing a fast-cycle organization, and maximizing performance in a wide-span organization.

In addition to the training geared for senior managers, open-enrollment courses (referred to as *Edge courses*) cover the same three content areas as the training for senior managers but in a more detailed fashion. Edge courses are designed for intact teams from mixed levels.

Analysis

Level 4. The course designer worked closely with Intel's president to determine the organization's current and future needs. The needs defined included decreasing cycle-time processes and managing successfully across organizations within Intel. Training designers established baselines for each area of improvement. The reward strategy was based on successful implementation of the program.

Level 3. Once the business-level indicators had been defined from the level 4 analyses, the environmental conditions and employee performance that needed to be changed in order to improve the business indicators were identified. Ensuring that all managers clearly understood expectations for improving business indicators was one of the critical environmental issues.

The training designer also determined that managers needed support when they returned to the workplace. To meet this need, Human Resources employees attended a three-day practitioner network training that included all the concepts that senior managers learned. The Human Resources employees acted as on-the-job coaches to the managers.

Level 2. Level 2 analysis determined a design for the training that would ensure the transfer of deficient skills and knowledge. Senior managers preferred lecture-based training, but the design needed also to include discussion groups, simulations, and case studies.

The training designer clarified course objectives and ensured that appropriate assessment and performance standards were identified for each objective. Level 2 evaluation was determined on the basis of the course objectives and the course design. The primary methods for level 2 evaluations are action plans and checklists.

Level 1. Level 1 analysis consisted of questions that assisted in designing instruction that would be at an appropriate skill level and motivating for participants. The analysis concluded that the instruction needed to be concise and to include high levels of interaction. To ensure that the entire senior training program was motivational, the designer built in fun activities both during the actual sessions and during the breaks. For example, in order to increase social networking and ensure that managers enjoyed themselves, one night event included karaoke.

The training designer established the minimum acceptable scores for level 1 through 3 evaluation during negotiations with the external training consultant. The external trainer had the responsibility of using the evaluation data to improve his performance.

Evaluation

Level 1. The level 1 evaluation consisted of a questionnaire for each day of the training session. Participants were asked about their reactions to the program design, materials, pacing, instructor, administration, and logistics. They were also asked if there were any barriers preventing them from using what they learned. The training developer used a scanner to tabulate the data.

The training developers used the resulting data to make several improvements. In one instance, the data showed that the instructor score was well below our defined standard. On the basis of this data, we replaced the external consultant who taught this section, but we retained the material that he was teaching. In another section, objective scores were low, but presentation scores were very high. The design team determined that the objectives had been written incorrectly. The evaluation scores improved as a result of course corrections.

Level 2. The level 2 evaluation consisted of demonstrating competency and creating action plans. Participants demonstrated their proficiency in group simulations and by creating action plans.

Their action plans needed to contain the specific steps that they would take to implement the concepts that they had learned within their organization. For example, a senior manager could define an action plan that included at least six different options. Examples of these options included sending groups of intact teams to the Edge program and consulting with Intel's Human Resources group to build in reinforcements and other support systems.

The results of the level 2 evaluation showed that all senior managers were able to complete their action plan successfully. The course instructor made midcourse corrections and used the checklist data to individualize instruction.

Level 3. The level 3 evaluations consisted of following up with the managers to determine whether they had met their action plans. (For example, did managers implement cycle-time reduction programs within their organization?) The data gathered during the level 3 analysis phase were used as a baseline. Data were also gathered on any environmental conditions that hindered performance.

Results showed that more than 70 percent of the managers followed through with their entire action plan. All managers did at least one item on their action plan. These data showed that, although there was some initial negative input on the level 1 evaluation, senior managers received sufficient support to transfer the key concepts back to the job.

The level 3 data, together with the level 4 data, were used as the early analysis for future interventions. The level 3 evaluations brought to light several issues specific to the organization that are now being worked by the organization's Human Resources group.

Level 4. Level 4 evaluation has been an ongoing process of tracking the business indicators defined during the initial analysis phase. One indicator is reduction of cycle time for key business processes. The total cost of developing and implementing the program was also calculated and used as comparison data with the business results.

The project thus far has shown favorable business results. Executives received bonus payouts based on the results.

The program sponsors and training consultants received a report on all the analysis and evaluation data gathered and on the recommendations that resulted.

Summary

By positioning the Kirkpatrick model as a methodology for analysis throughout the instructional systems design process, Intel Corporation has been able to improve the process for needs assessment, design, and evaluation and demonstrate the impact of training on business indicators.

Chapter 12

Evaluating the Creative
Manager Training Program

The evaluating of training is so important at Motorola that
Motorola University has a separate department that is specifically for that purpose on a worldwide basis. The department
is managed by Dave Basarab, who contributed the foreword to
this book. This case study describes the process and results for
evaluating at levels 1, 2, and 3. The sophisticated design that
it outlines will interest any organization that takes evaluation
seriously.

Motorola Corporation

Dave Basarab, Manager of Evaluation
Motorola University, Schaumberg, Illinois

Introduction

Every year, Motorola invests more than 4.4 million hours of employee time and more than 200 million dollars in training. With
this kind of investment, the business portions of Motorola asked
Motorola University (a corporate entity) for help in determining whether the money invested in training results in the performance expected on the job. To address their concern, Motorola
University formed the Evaluation Department.

This department functions as a central source for the processing of training evaluation data from around the world. More than sixty-five Motorola training departments are currently served, with locations including China, Korea, Malaysia, Japan, the United Kingdom, Phoenix, Chicago, Austin, and greater Boston. The Evaluation department is composed of a full-time staff dedicated to consultation on evaluation procedures and to the processing and reporting of evaluation information.

Motorola University has adopted the Kirkpatrick model for training evaluation, but it has added its own unique focus to the effort. We define evaluation as a systematic process to collect data and convert those data into usable information. Training evaluation information is used to improve training programs, measure the effects of training, help in decision making, determine and track the quality of training, and act on the results. Motorola's use of the four Kirkpatrick evaluation levels is shown in Table 12.1.

Table 12.1. Motorola's Evaluation Levels

Evaluation Level	Kirkpatrick Definition	Motorola's Use
Level 1	Reaction	Customer satisfaction index from participants
Level 2	Learning	Mastery of knowledge and skills
Level 3	Behavior	Application of knowledge and skills on the job
Level 4	Results	Organizational impact

We use a systematic process to evaluate training at all levels. The process consists of specific steps and criteria to follow when conducting an evaluation study. It is much more than a map. It is a guide complete with process specifications and examples that help users to plan, develop, collect, analyze, and report various types of evaluation data at all levels. It is flexible enough to walk you through a simple descriptive analysis and detailed enough to guide you through advanced causal comparative and correlational studies. The process used at Motorola is shown in Figure 12.1.

Figure 12.1. Motorola's Evaluation Process

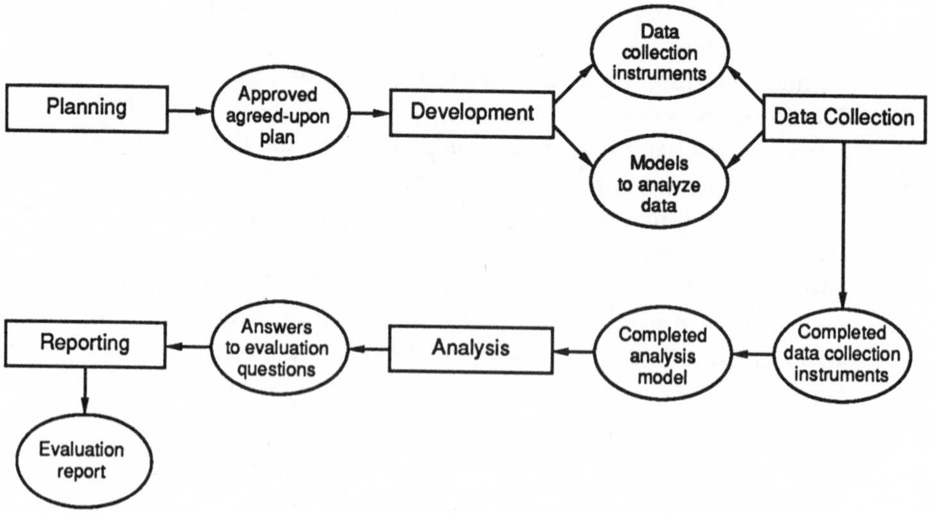

The Creative Manager

The evaluation of a program called The Creative Manager illustrates Motorola's evaluation process. The three-day program was designed, developed, and delivered by Motorola University throughout the world. It focuses on a manager's ability to recognize and develop the creative potential in himself or herself and in others by applying the creative process to generate, develop, and champion unique ideas.

Participants in this skill-based course not only develop new definitions of creativity but also assess their own innate creative potential, apply an eight-step creative process to various topics, and develop their ability to use creative techniques to generate ideas. The target audience for this course is all Motorola managers and team leaders.

The program has three goals: to develop creative behaviors, to apply the creative process to various topics, and to learn and use tools that can develop creativity in oneself and in others.

Planning the Evaluation

The evaluation process calls for the identification and interviewing of evaluation stakeholders—individuals who have a vested interest in the training and its outcomes. The primary stakeholder for this evaluation was the manager of the Motorola University competency center for management education. She was interviewed to determine the purpose of the evaluation and the intended use of its results, her commitment to the evaluation, any constraints on data collection and observation, on-the-job performance goals and expectations, organizational issues that may inhibit performance, any significant issues affecting performance, evaluation study time frames, report format, whether the study was aimed at the discovery of possible causes for behavior transfer, and whether we needed to explore the magnitude of the relationship between two variables.

After the interviews, an evaluation plan was written and signed by the stakeholder. The plan stated that the purpose of the evaluation was to determine what the participants liked and disliked about the training (level 1 evaluation), the learning that occurred because of the training (level 2 evaluation), and the degree to which participants have successfully transferred skills learned in the course to their jobs (level 3 evaluation).

The information collected was used in two ways: to identify and correct problems associated with the training and thereby improve the program (formative evaluation) and to verify the worth and merit of the training itself (summative evaluation).

Developing the Data Collection
Instruments and Analysis Models

This phase of the evaluation process develops the data collection instruments and analysis models (tools used to summarize the data) specified in the evaluation plan. According to the plan, we built instruments for three levels.

Level 1

Level 1 evaluation at Motorola studies the satisfaction of participants with the training event. The Participant Assessment (PA)
form was used to capture level 1 evaluation data on participants'
overall satisfaction with course relevancy, design, perceived learning, instructor performance, materials, and learning environment.
Data collected from the Participant Assessment form are completely anonymous.

The individual items on the Participant Assessment form assess the following: relevancy (items 1–4), perceived learning (item
5), course design (items 6–13), instructor (items 14–20), training
facility (item 21), printed materials (item 22), and overall satisfaction (item 23). Each response on the Participant Assessment
form is considered as falling into one of the following three
categories: satisfied, dissatisfied, or null (neither satisfied nor dissatisfied).

From these responses, we calculate a customer satisfaction percentage for each item, each category of items, and the entire assessment. This is the formula:

$$\text{Customer satisfaction} = \left(\frac{\text{Satisfied responses}}{\text{Total responses} - \text{Null responses}} \right) \times 100$$

A training session has met the quality goal if customer satisfaction meets or exceeds 90 percent for each category of responses
(relevancy, course design, instructor, and so on). If the training
session is considered a pilot, the course is released if it meets or
exceeds 80 percent customer satisfaction in the categories of
relevancy and course design.

The Motorola University Evaluation Department uses a customer system called AdEPT (*Ad*vanced *E*valuation *P*articipant
*T*echnology) as its analysis model in support of its training
evaluation activities. AdEPT is an automated system that allows
Motorola University to gather level 1 and level 2 evaluation data
and provide reports to its clients. The gathering and reporting
of level 1 and level 2 evaluation data can be used to improve a
course during its design, development, and initial implementation or to pinpoint opportunities for improvement after the course
has been implemented. The primary benefit to Motorola Univer-

sity and its clients is timely access to data that provide a starting point for improving the quality of training.

Level 2

Level 2 evaluation is known at Motorola University as the *mastery assessment process*. The mastery assessment process determines the effectiveness of a course in providing participants with the knowledge and skills prescribed by the objectives. Level 2 data are used to evaluate courses, not personnel. In other words, data collected by giving tests are used to look for patterns within the results so that action plans to improve learning can be implemented. The data collected are not used to grade participants, imply passing or failing a course, or provide input for participants' performance reviews.

Quality goals are documented during development, and evaluation data are collected on training sessions that are reported to evaluation clients. The heart of the mastery assessment process is called the *mastery matrix of learning*. Table 12.2 shows the mastery matrix of learning for the Creative Manager program.

Table 12.2. Mastery Matrix of
Learning for the Creative Manager Program

Objective Being Evaluated	Test Number	Mastery Score	Lower Control Limit
1	1	80%	77%
2	2	80	77
3	3	80	77
4	4	80	77
5	5	80	77

Note: Quality goal: 80 percent of the participants score at or above the lower control limit for each objective; N = 2,000

The matrix concept allows the designer to select the objectives that are to be evaluated, the tests used to collect data on learning, and the minimum test score that a participant needs to obtain in order to indicate mastery of an objective. To take into account that people learn differently and take tests differently and that instructors teach differently (together, these differences are known as *process variation*), we calculate a lower control limit for each test. This value estimates three standard deviations below the mastery score for a population of a given size. This value then accounts for any process variation in the instructional event. This is the formula used for calculating the lower control limit:

$$LCL = P - 3\sqrt{\frac{P(1-P)}{n}}$$

where LCL = lower control limit, P = defined mastery score, and n = the number of people to be trained. A training session meets the quality criterion if 80 percent of the participants score at or above the lower control limit on all tests. The quality goal must be achieved at pilot test for the course to be released.

Level 2 evaluation data are captured by administering the Motorola University mastery assessment to all students as specified in the course's instructor guide.

Level 3

Level 3 evaluation at Motorola is a process that collects data to determine whether the skills learned in training are being applied on the job or, if they are not, why and to identify the training, cultural, and organizational issues that may inhibit application of the skills learned.

For the Creative Manager course, participants provided the names of three associates who would be able to comment on their effective use of the creative process. A follow-up survey regarding behavioral transfer was mailed to the particpants and the associates whom they named. The first fifty participants who attended the Creative Manager program were surveyed in an attempt to answer the following evaluation questions:

1. Has the participant exhibited the behaviors learned in the course on the job? If the answer is yes, how often were the behaviors exhibited?
2. Did the participant perceive the results of his or her behaviors to be positive or negative?

3. Does the participant feel that the behaviors that he or she exhibited should be continued?
4. If the skills were exhibited more than once, did the participant feel that improvement occurred as a result of training (if applicable)?
5. Did environmental influences help or hinder the use of the skills on the job?
6. Does the participant consider the creative manager program to be valuable for teaching and promoting the components of creativity, traits, idea-finding techniques, and the creative problem-solving process?

A second survey was administered to the 150 coworkers whom they had identified as people who would have an opportunity to observe their use of creative skills and behaviors within ninety days of training. Responses from this survey were used to answer the following evaluation questions:

1. Have associates observed the participant exhibiting the behaviors learned in the course on the job? If behaviors were observed, how often were they observed? If behaviors were not observed, is it the associate's perception that the participant had the opportunity to exhibit the behaviors taught in the course?
2. Did associates perceive the results of the participant's behaviors to be positive or negative?
3. Do associates feel that the participant's behaviors should be continued?
4. If the skills were exhibited more than once, did associates feel that improvement occurred as a result of training (if applicable)?

Collecting Evaluation Data

The data collection phase of the Motorola University training evaluation process involves the gathering of data to address the evaluation questions posed in the evaluation plan. Data sources include people, documents, and performance data. The data collection effort for the creative manager program followed the timetable shown in Figure 12.2.

Figure 12.2. Evaluation Data Collection Timetable

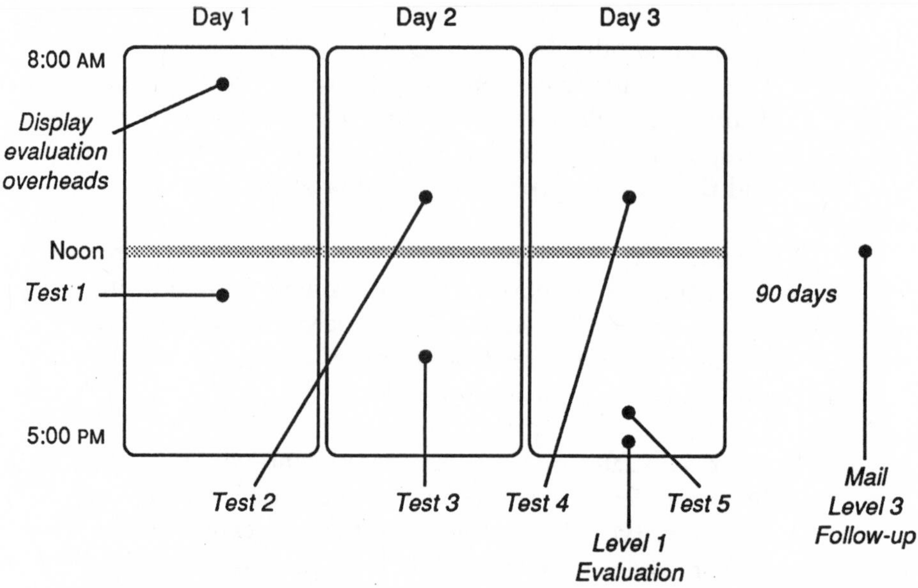

Level 1 and level 2 evaluation data were collected for all classes. One level 3 data collection was conducted.

Analyzing the Data

In the analysis phase, the data collected are interpreted. This phase answers the evaluation questions posed in the evaluation plan. Figures 12.3 through 12.5 show the results for the Creative Manager program by evaluation level.

Reporting the Results

The purpose of reporting results is to communicate training evaluation information to stakeholders and interested audiences so they

Figure 12.3. Level 1: Customer Satisfaction

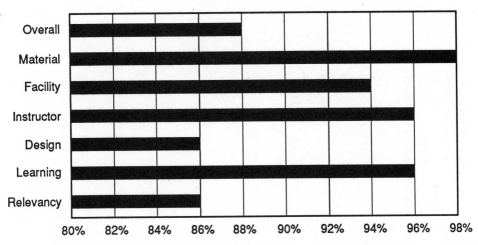

Note: N = 211

can use the information for decision making. Table 12.3 shows the reporting structure for level 1 and level 2 data from the Creative Manager program. Reports were distributed through electronic mail.

Twenty-eight of the fifty participants who attended the Creative Manager training completed and returned the survey designed to collect level 3 data. Of the 149 associates identified by participants, 102 people completed and returned the survey.

Overall, the majority of the training participants and their associates felt that the skills and traits of creativity were being used on the job. However, agreement between training participants and their associates was not reached when they were asked about the job circumstances under which the skills and traits of creativity were being applied. Significantly more participants than associates reported that the participants were using the skills and traits in each circumstance.

Both groups surveyed agreed that the results of displaying the skills and traits were generally positive.

Regarding organizational influences on the use of the skills and traits of creativity, more than half of the participants agreed that employee recognition programs (71 percent), availability of re-

Figure 12.4. Level 2: Mastery of Objectives

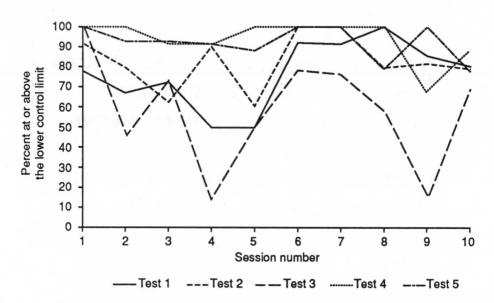

Figure 12.5. Level 3: Application of Skills on the Job

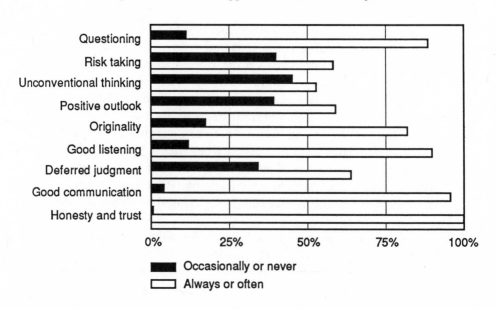

Table 12.3. Reporting Structure, Level 1 and Level 2 Data

Report	Frequency	Purpose
Level 1		
Weekly report	Every Thursday	Provides a summary report of customer satisfaction for all training sessions in the preceding week
Monthly report	First two business days of the month	Summarizes the distribution of responses to the target audience question, by course, for the preceding month
Quarterly report (management summary)	First two business days of the quarter	Summarizes the results of responses to items dealing with instructor performance, by instructor, for the preceding quarter
Level 2		
Weekly report	Every Thursday	Provides a summary report on achievement of the learning quality goal for all sessions
Learning history	Every Thursday for each session where learning quality is below goal and on demand	Documents all learning throughout the life of the course, helps to determine root cause when quality has not been achieved

sources (54 percent), and personal attitudes and values (75 percent) helped them back on the job. Hindrances to using the skills and traits included organizational, social, and political attitudes (56 percent).

Overall, 96 percent of the participants found the training program to be of value to them on the job.

Chapter 13

Evaluating an Outdoor-Based Training Program

The research described in this case study evaluated both level 1, reaction, and level 3, behavior. It is unique for three reasons. First, it evaluates an outdoor-based training program, not the usual classroom course. Second, the results are analyzed statistically to determine the significance of any change observed. Third, evaluation led to a number of recommendations for future programs.

St. Luke's Hospital

Richard Wagner, Assistant Professor of Management
University of Wisconsin, Whitewater

Robert Weigand, Manager, Training and Development
St. Luke's Hospital, Bethlehem, Pennsylvania

The Program

Faced with increasing competition from nearby hospitals and the need to improve efficiency and cost control, St. Luke's Hospital began to look for innovative ways of improving its training of management personnel. In 1990, St. Luke's Training Department, with the support of top management, introduced the concept of outdoor-based training. While outdoor-based training programs for the training of managers are relatively recent, they have been found to be effective in improving interdepartmental communications, increasing the level of trust among employees, and empowering employees at all levels by reducing existing boundaries between departments.

St. Luke's Hospital, a 435-bed medical complex located in the Lehigh Valley of Pennsylvania, began using outdoor-based training as a technique for training management personnel in 1990. While those who attended the early programs expressed a great deal of satisfaction with them, no formal evaluation of these programs had been conducted.

The use of outdoor-based training programs at St. Luke's was supported by top management primarily as a means of improving interdepartmental communications. The primary goals were to make interdepartmental communications more direct and to increase the honesty and openness of such communications. Additional goals of the program were to increase the level of trust among employees, to empower employees at all levels by encouraging increased sharing, and to reduce the boundaries that existed between departments within the hospital.

The outdoor-based experiential training program was conducted in three one-day phases at a remote location called Stony Acres. Program participants were management employees from areas throughout the hospital, including human resources, accounting, engineering, and a number of medical departments. All participants were volunteers. A key feature of the program was that each of the groups traveled to and from the training site in a bus together. This feature served to increase the informal interaction and communication between group members.

Phase I of the training program focused on having the participants get to know one another better as individuals, to begin to improve interpersonal communications, and to work on some initial trust issues between employees. "Low ropes" activities were used in the morning. These activities included the wall, in which the group has to climb a twelve-foot-high wall using only its own resources; the spider's web, where the group has to pass all members through a rope web without disturbing the "spider"; and the blind trust walk, where the group is blindfolded and led on a walk through the woods. In the afternoon, the group was led through three "high ropes" activities. In high ropes activities, the events take place from ten to twenty feet above the ground. The overall mix of activities for the program was approximately 60 percent low elements and 40 percent high elements.

Phase II focused on building trust and group support by increasing the level of challenge for participants. The morning session began with a warm-up session to get the participants ready for the rest of the day. The morning also focused on building trust and on developing a challenge by choice contract so that no one felt pressures to participate in the high ropes activities. The afternoon was devoted to the high ropes activities and to building group trust through group support. The mix for this phase of the program was approximately 40 percent low elements and 60 percent high elements.

Phase III focused on individual development and increasing group support. The mix for this phase of the program was about 25 percent low ropes and trust building and 75 percent high ropes and individual development.

The processing or debriefing of each activity by a skilled facilitator has been found to be a key element in the effective transfer of training material to the work setting. In order to maximize the transfer of training, it was decided to use two debriefing periods: one by the facilitator after each activity during the program and another during a follow-up program after each phase had been completed. The feeling of group spirit and togetherness was further fostered by the use of group T-shirts and group slogans.

The Evaluation

In 1991, an effort to evaluate the effectiveness of outdoor-based training was undertaken by Robert Weigand, St. Luke's manager of training and development, and Richard J. Wagner, assistant professor of management at the University of Wisconsin, Whitewater. As manager of training and development, Bob Weigand had directed the design of the outdoor-based program and was its primary facilitator. Dick Wagner, a former corporate training director, currently serves as a consultant to a number of major organizations on evaluation of their experiential training programs. The evaluation program designed for St. Luke's combined the unique features of its program with the quantitative evaluation format that Wagner and his associates had used elsewhere.

Part I of the evaluation program was designed to develop a "theory" of what the Stony Acres program accomplished for those who had participated in it. While St. Luke's top management had established the goals of the program, there was no way to be sure that these goals were all that this type of program was accomplishing. Since subject matter experts—a group of previous participants—existed, Wiegand and Wagner felt that they could offer some unique insights into the program before they began to evaluate new participants. Due to the geography of the evaluation, a nondirectional questionnaire was used to gather these data. The questionnaire asked participants to describe what they had personally gotten out of the Stony Acres program and how it had changed their behaviors at work.

The results of this survey suggested that participation was associated with a number of behavioral changes that program designers had not anticipated. An analysis of these surveys by a four-member panel of the research team indicated that these behaviors could be grouped into four categories: communications, team spirit, willingness to try new ideas, and interpersonal relations. A questionnaire was then developed to allow the researchers to evaluate the responses of future participants to the program.

In part II of the evaluation program, the instrument developed in part I was given to participants in the second program. The participants completed the evaluation instrument at three different times: before attending phase I, three months after completing phase III, and six months after completing the program. In an effort to improve the precision of the evaluation and to focus on the actual results of the program, participants completed an open-response questionnaire on behavior style three months after the program to justify any behavioral changes that they felt had taken place after the program. Since this questionnaire was tied directly to the program, it was felt that three months was both long enough to reduce the typical euphoria after training and short enough that participants would remember the specifics of the Stony Acres program. Exhibit 13.1 shows the questionnaire administered three months after training.

Part III of the evaluation consisted of a questionnaire administered before training and six months after training. The questionnaire used items developed during previous research in similar programs. Since all these items are behavioral, administering the instrument six months after training made it possible to evaluate the long-term impact of outdoor training on these behaviors. In addition to the scale developed specifically for the Stony Acres program, the instrument measured five other behaviors: *Group trust* measured the extent to which the participants was willing to assign good intentions to and have confidence in the words and actions of his or her coworkers. *Self-esteem* assessed whether the participant had a positive or negative view of him- or her self (a measure of the participant's self-confidence). *Group awareness* measured the feeling among group members that each member of the group recognized the differences in abilities between the individual members of the group and understood and was committed to the group's goals. *Group effectiveness* was seen as the best measure of the overall functioning of the group, including the level of cooperation, the effectiveness of communications within the group, and the group's clarity about its goals. *Group bonding* was seen as a broad measure of group cohesiveness; this behavior included group stimulation, group commitment, and group compatibility.

In addition to behaviors, the questionnaires also measured participants' attitudes toward the Stony Acres program. The attitudes measured included participants' general feeling toward the program and what they would tell other people about the program if asked. Exhibit 13.2 shows the attitude/behavioral questionnaire.

Results of Evaluation

A total of sixteen managers, seven males and nine females, completed the Stony Acres program. The average age of the participants

Exhibit 13.1. St. Luke's Theory Questionnaire

Please answer each of the following questions using the following scale:

1 = Increased strongly after outdoor training
2 = Increased moderately after outdoor training
3 = Increased slightly after outdoor training
4 = Did not change after outdoor training
5 = Decreased slightly after outdoor training
6 = Decreased moderately after outdoor training
7 = Decreased strongly after outdoor training

After you have rated a statement, briefly describe a specific situation that justifies your rating.

1. I find this group to be very friendly. _____
   Justification:

2. I think communications in this group need a lot of help. _____
   Justification:

3. There is a lot of team spirit in this group. _____
   Justification:

4. This is a very informal and relaxed group to be with. _____
   Justification:

5. The members of this group are very willing to help each other solve problems. _____
   Justification:

6. As a group, we communicate really well with each other. _____
   Justification:

7. The members of this group really know each other as individuals. _____
   Justification:

8. I am more willing to try new ideas because I know that the members of this group will help me if I need it. _____
   Justification:

9. The members of this group carefully guard their territory. _____
   Justification:

10. The members of this group are open and easy to get to know. _____
    Justification:

Exhibit 13.2. St. Luke's Attitude/Behavioral Questionnaire

Sex: Male   Female   (circle one)

Age: _____ .

Education: High school grad   Attended some college

College grad   Tech school grad

Graduate degree   No high school diploma

(Circle the highest level completed)

General Instructions

This survey contains a number of questions about you and your job. All the questions ask that you choose the one number that best matches the description of how you feel about the question. Please mark only *one* box.

The following statements concern your perceptions of the Outdoor-Based Training Program (OBT) that you will attend shortly. How much do you agree or disagree with each of the following statements?

1 = Disagree strongly
2 = Disagree moderately
3 = Disagree slightly
4 = Neither agree nor disagree
5 = Agree slightly
6 = Agree moderately
7 = Agree strongly

I understand completely the objectives of the OBT.	1 2 3 4 5 6 7
I can see no potential value in the OBT.	1 2 3 4 5 6 7
I have no idea what you do in the OBT.	1 2 3 4 5 6 7
I am very much looking forward to participating in the OBT.	1 2 3 4 5 6 7
I would strongly prefer not to participate in the OBT.	1 2 3 4 5 6 7
I think that the OBT is a great idea for improving effectiveness at my organization.	1 2 3 4 5 6 7
I have heard good things about the OBT.	1 2 3 4 5 6 7

Please circle the one that best describes you at *work*.

Successful	1 2 3 4 5 6 7	Not successful
Important	1 2 3 4 5 6 7	Not important
Doing my best	1 2 3 4 5 6 7	Not doing my best
Happy	1 2 3 4 5 6 7	Not happy

Exhibit 13.2. St. Luke's Attitude/Behavioral Questionnaire *(continued)*

How much do you agree or disagree with each of the following statements?

1 = Disagree strongly
2 = Disagree moderately
3 = Disagree slightly
4 = Neither agree nor disagree
5 = Agree slightly
6 = Agree moderately
7 = Agree strongly

If I get into difficulties at work, I know that my workmates would try to help me out.	1 2 3 4 5 6 7
I can trust the people with whom I work to lend me a hand if I need it.	1 2 3 4 5 6 7
Most of my workmates can be relied upon to do as they say they will do.	1 2 3 4 5 6 7
I have full confidence in the skills of my workmates.	1 2 3 4 5 6 7
Most of my fellow workers would get on the job even if supervisors were not around.	1 2 3 4 5 6 7
I can rely on other workers not to make my job more difficult by careless work.	1 2 3 4 5 6 7
I recognize that members of my work group vary widely in skills and abilities.	1 2 3 4 5 6 7
I recognize that my work group contains members from widely varying backgrounds.	1 2 3 4 5 6 7
My work group knows exactly what things it has to get done.	1 2 3 4 5 6 7
Each member of my work group has a clear idea of the group's goals.	1 2 3 4 5 6 7
I feel that I am really a part of my work group.	1 2 3 4 5 6 7
I look forward to being with the members of my work group each day.	1 2 3 4 5 6 7
To what extent does your work group plan together and coordinate efforts?	1 2 3 4 5 6 7
To what extent does your work group make good decisions and solve problems well?	1 2 3 4 5 6 7
To what extent do persons in your work group know what their jobs are and how to do them well?	1 2 3 4 5 6 7

Exhibit 13.2. St. Luke's Attitude/Behavioral Questionnaire *(continued)*

To what extent is information about important events and situations shared within your work group?   1 2 3 4 5 6 7

To what extent does your work group really want to meet its objectives successfully?   1 2 3 4 5 6 7

To what extent is your work group able to respond to unusual work demands placed upon it?   1 2 3 4 5 6 7

To what extent do you have confidence and trust in the persons in your work group?   1 2 3 4 5 6 7

Please answer the following questions about your feelings towards the group with which you attended *OBT.*

> 1 = Disagree strongly
> 2 = Disagree moderately
> 3 = Disagree slightly
> 4 = Neither agree nor disagree
> 5 = Agree slightly
> 6 = Agree moderately
> 7 = Agree strongly

I have influenced what the group talked about and did.   1 2 3 4 5 6 7

I have felt excited in this group.   1 2 3 4 5 6 7

I think about the group between sessions.   1 2 3 4 5 6 7

I am included by the group in the group's activities.   1 2 3 4 5 6 7

I have regretted joining this group.   1 2 3 4 5 6 7

I would not mind missing future training sessions with this group.   1 2 3 4 5 6 7

I think that the group should meet more often.   1 2 3 4 5 6 7

I want to remain in the group.   1 2 3 4 5 6 7

I would like the opportunity to dissuade members if most of the members decided to dissolve the group by leaving.   1 2 3 4 5 6 7

Most of the members fit what I feel to be the idea of a good group member.   1 2 3 4 5 6 7

I find the activities in which I participate as a member of the group to be enjoyable.   1 2 3 4 5 6 7

The group is composed of people who fit together.   1 2 3 4 5 6 7

I like the group that I am in.   1 2 3 4 5 6 7

Exhibit 13.2. St. Luke's Attitude/Behavioral Questionnaire *(continued)*

Please answer the following questions about your feelings toward the group with which you attended *OBT*.

> 1 = Disagree strongly
> 2 = Disagree moderately
> 3 = Disagree slightly
> 4 = Neither agree nor disagree
> 5 = Agree slightly
> 6 = Agree moderately
> 7 = Agree strongly

I find this group to be very friendly.	1 2 3 4 5 6 7
I think that communications in this group need a lot of help.	1 2 3 4 5 6 7
There is a lot of team spirit in this group.	1 2 3 4 5 6 7
This is a very informal and relaxed group to be with.	1 2 3 4 5 6 7
The members of this group are very willing to help each other solve problems.	1 2 3 4 5 6 7
As a group, we communicate really well with each other.	1 2 3 4 5 6 7
The members of this group really know each other as individuals.	1 2 3 4 5 6 7
I am more willing to try new ideas because I know that the members of this group will help me if I need it.	1 2 3 4 5 6 7
The members of this group carefully guard their territory.	1 2 3 4 5 6 7
The members of this group are open and easy to get to know.	1 2 3 4 5 6 7

---

was 39.8 years old, with the youngest being twenty-five and the oldest sixty-one. Six were high school graduates, four had some college, and the remaining six were college graduates.

St. Luke's Theory Measures

The results of empirical evaluation of the behavioral changes measured with the St. Luke's theory measures instrument at three months showed statistically significant changes in all four behaviors (communications, team spirit, willingness to try new ideas, and interpersonal relations). After six months, a significant change was found only in communications. Table 13.1 shows the statistics.

Table 13.1. St. Luke's Theory Measures

Measure	Before Training	Six Months After Training	Change Before to Six Months After	Change After Three Months
Communications	4.33 (1.267)	5.42 (1.475)	+1.08ᵃ	+2.73ᵃ
Team spirit	5.17 (.835)	5.33 (1.231)	+.17	+2.00ᵃ
Willingness to try new ideas	4.42 (1.676)	5.08 (1.730)	+.67	+2.47ᵃ
Interpersonal relations	4.81 (.912)	4.89 (1.301)	+.08	+2.42ᵃ

Note: ᵃ$p < .05$ (the change was statistically significant); $N = 16$.

Behavioral Justifications

The results of the behavioral justification questionnaires suggest that the participants could link the training program to specific actions at work. Exhibit 13.3 summarizes the behavioral justifications received from participants by category.

Previous Research Measures

The results of the empirical evaluation of reactions to the program after six months showed that, overall, participants' attitude toward the program was more favorable than it had been before the program (remember, they all volunteered) but that the increase was not statistically significant. Of the five behaviors that were evaluated, only one, group effectiveness, showed a significant improvement. Table 13.2 shows the statistics.

Conclusions

One major difficulty in analyzing outdoor-based training programs like the Stony Acres program has been the absence of agreement

Exhibit 13.3. Behavioral Justifications

Communications

- Communications with certain individuals with whom I often interact improved, but I only interact with some group members.
- Being physically close during training improved communication.
- After Stony Acres, we are more relaxed around each other and communicate better. Less formality makes communication easier.
- We had communication problems on one activity but learned from it.
- After the program, I feel comfortable speaking to upper management.
- Each activity saw communications improve as defenses came down, each member gave input, and we learned to listen better.
- Open communications have continued into the work setting.
- Some people now communicate with me more at work than before training.
- A few challenges really helped to improve communications.
- We are more confident is speaking with each other on issues that affect us.
- Everyone could express an opinion without criticism.

Team spirit

- Follow-up meeting was fun. We worked together to design our T-shirts.
- The procedures for each challenge built this up.
- As the day went on, the group became more relaxed with each other and had more fun being together.
- I am amazed at how positive people react to this type of training.
- Going over the wall really increased our team spirit.
- Best example was going over the wall.
- We could see it grow throughout the day, even if it started high.
- The challenge of completing the spider web really brought everyone together.

Try new ideas

- This increased due to collaborative problem solving.
- We all became committed to doing the best that we can with the support of the others.
- Absolutely, because I trust them.
- During training, I got to know some upper managers better, and I would now consult them for help.

Interpersonal relations

- Positive hallway interaction
- More socializing
- During training, everyone distanced themselves from the work hierarchy.
- After training, people are free to visit other people's territory.
- Training allowed people to be more informal.
- At work, we are more open with each other.

Exhibit 13.3. Behavioral Justifications *(continued)*

- When different levels of management are out of the office setting, they were able to interact and joke around with each other.
- Now everyone says hello to each other.
- Some members still guard their territory very closely.
- The ride to the site was in their clique but not the ride home.
- At the end of the day, everyone could relax and laugh about the comments made about you—both positive and negative.
- Met new people and got to know old acquaintances better.
- Secret friend discussing made me feel more open with others.
- Territorial boundaries have come down.
- Talking and laughing really helps.
- Lunch was very relaxed. Everyone shared food.
- Learned individual fears.
- Relations with other group members improved during the session and have continued to get better since that time.
- Group worked together to complete each challenge.
- Apprehensive group members were more willing to help each other by the end of the day.
- People became more relaxed with each other as the day went on.
- A hello and a smile go a long way.
- Formal barriers have been reduced and even eliminated.

Table 13.2. Previous Research Measures

Measure	Before Mean/SD	Six Months After Mean/SD	t	p value
Attitude toward program	5.18 (.960)	5.64 (1.214)	1.20	.257
Trust in group members	5.78 (.780)	5.77 (.875)	0.06	.957
Self-esteem	2.10 (1.068)	2.38 (1.408)	0.79	.445
Group awareness	5.90 (.754)	5.97 (.807)	0.48	.643
Group effectiveness	4.06 (.473)	5.81 (1.212)	6.26	.000*
Group bonding	4.62 (.851)	4.99 (1.106)	0.85	.413

Note: $p < .05$ (the change was statistically significant); $N = 16$

on the goals of such programs. Part I of the evaluation program described in this case study attempted to develop a "theory" of what should happen during the Stony Acres program by asking prior participants to tell what they thought had happened as a result of attending the program. It should be noted that these participants had all expressed strongly positive feelings about the Stony Acres program. The behaviors that they identified focused on areas that the researchers had observed to be keys to the effectiveness of outdoor-based programs.

The results of the questionnaire administered three months after the program suggest that significant changes occurred in the behaviors identified in part I. It was not surprising that participants reported strongly positive behavior changes as the result of the program three months after training. Anecdotal evidence strongly suggests that participants in general really enjoy programs like Stony Acres. Thus, posttraining euphoria suggests that, when asked directly, participants in a program of this nature would say that it had been very effective.

However, the behavioral justifications that participants gave for their behavior change ratings strongly support the direction (if not the magnitude) of the behavior change ratings that they identified after three months. In the area of communications, ten of the sixteen participants gave a specific example of a positive change that had occurred after the program. Only one participant had concern—that the participant did not interact with the other members of the group on a regular basis.

In the area of team spirit, nine of the sixteen participants described a specific positive change in their behavior. In the area of trying new ideas, only five of the sixteen participants referred to a specific behavioral change that had occurred, but all five were positive. Finally, in the area of interpersonal relations, all sixteen participants referred to specifics. One was negative, and the remaining fifteen were strongly positive. In fact, almost half of the participants described having seen more than one specific behavioral change after the program.

By asking participants to rate only their behaviors, not their behavior changes, the questionnaire administered six months after training was subject to little if any posttraining euphoria. Thus, the findings from this portion of the part II study can be viewed as a more conservative estimate of the effectiveness of the Stony Acres program. After six months, only communications showed a statistically significant improvement. While a relatively large improvement was also found in willingness to try new ideas (.67), this change was not statistically significant, primarily due to the small sample size ($N = 16$).

The results of evaluation after six months indicate only one statistically significant change: in group effectiveness. It is interesting from an organizational perspective that group effectiveness is the behavior measure most closely linked to actual job performance and work output. A large positive change was also found in group bonding, but the small sample size ($N = 16$) kept this change from being statistically significant.

While the results after six months indicated no significant change in two measures in which researchers have generally found changes — trust in group members and group awareness — the improvement in group effectiveness had not been predicted by past research. We believe that two conditions may explain these unexpected results: Participants were not from an intact work group, and participants were from a service-based industry. Most of the research in this area has been done in production and research environments, not in service-oriented organizations.

Intact work teams have generally shown significant improvements in group interaction measures but not in group effectiveness. Groups that are not intact work teams seldom show improvements in group interaction measures, but they may show improvements in the overall measure of group effectiveness.

Work groups in service-based industries seem to have higher levels of trust and group awareness, but they are generally less task oriented before attending the outdoor-based training program. Thus, since service industry groups already have high levels of trust and group awareness, these measures may show only small improvements during the training programs. However, since service industry groups are not strongly task oriented before they attend training, this key area may improve significantly during the training program. Production and research groups may experience the opposite reaction: little change in task-oriented behaviors, since these are already high, and significant change in group awareness and trust, since these are relatively low prior to training.

Comments

The goals of the evaluation described in this case study were to determine the impact of an outdoor-based training program on organizationally desired behaviors and to determine whether modifications to the program could improve its effectiveness. The results of the study indicate that the Stony Acres program was effective in achieving some of its goals and that these changes persist over relatively long periods of time. The evaluation of the program suggests that participants have a positive reaction to the program, experience positive behavioral changes as a result of the program, and can link these changes to actual results on the job.

Several changes in the Stony Acres program are being considered as a direct result of the ongoing evaluation process. First, an indoor-based program needs to be available for the people who do not want to participate in the outdoor program. An indoor program carefully designed to match the "learning" goals and process of the Stony Acres program is scheduled to begin soon. A second change now under consideration is in the overall structure of the program. Interviews with participants after the program suggest that the sequence of the program needs to change and that the program needs to include other, indoor, nonexperiential training. This would mean that the outdoor, experiential components of the Stony Acres program might become a part of a larger program and serve as hands-on examples of such activities as problem solving and group communications. Participants in this larger program might participate in Stony Acres phase I, then attend a more traditional training program, and follow up with the other phases of Stony Acres, intermixed with traditional training activities.

Chapter 14

IBM Takes the
Guessing Out of Testing

In order to add a new dimension to level 2 (learning), evaluators at IBM added a confidence index (CI) that asked participants to indicate the level of confidence that they had for their answers to a test. The test was a true-or-false test with a hundred items. After answering each item, the participant circled a number indicating his or her level of confidence in the answer: 1 = reasonably sure, 2 = not sure but probably, and 3 = don't know. The test was given twice, before and after training, and the answers were compared. Results of the testing were analyzed on a statistical basis.

IBM Corporation

George M. Alliger, Assistant Professor
State University of New York, Albany

Harold M. Horowitz, President, HRM Associates
former Program Director,
Instructional Applications Research, IBM

Measuring how effectively training satisfies corporate goals is a major challenge for training and development specialists. Many training programs have no assessment mechanisms to determine their quantitative effectiveness. Instructors typically solicit the opinions of the students. They ask, "Did this course meet its stated objectives?" or "Did you enjoy this course?" but "happiness-sheet" feedback hardly answers the crucial question, "Are the students learning anything?" To answer that question, trainers must measure knowledge gain and retention.

In 1985, IBM's internal education organization began a programmatic research effort to find out whether new, internally developed training technologies increased knowledge transfer and retention. In an experimental course, the organization successfully developed and implemented a unique method of knowledge testing, employing pre- and post-tests. The testing goes beyond reaction measurement (Kirkpatrick's Step One) and also provides more information than that gained from knowledge testing (Step Two).

Instrument Construction

A six-hour experimental course, designed to make maximum use of new training technologies, was the initial target for the new program of knowledge measurement. The course designers separated the course objectives into ten main segments; each segment encompassed, on average, ten key learning points. From that material, 100 content-valid, true-or-false questions were written. The course designers took great care to write questions that were challenging but fair, and relevant to the learning points and course objectives. In fact, the designers' goal was to create, when possible, questions that were "mini-case-studies" — that is, questions that required some situational analysis as well as knowledge of a principle or idea. In addition, the designers compared the learning points with the questions to ensure that the questions thoroughly covered the course's ten knowledge areas and the learning points within each area.

After extensive experiments with the questions to obtain estimates of difficulty, the designers created two nonoverlapping, parallel families of tests (four tests per family). Each test contained twenty-five questions, balanced according to the knowledge areas. Because of the particular circumstances, the designers considered that multiple forms of the test were important, not only to ensure differences between pre- and post-test questions, but also to minimize the ability of instructors to "teach to the test" instead of teaching the course as designed. In the same way, particular circumstances (such as time constraints) dictated the choice of the true/false format and the number of questions.

Trainees could answer each question, of course, either correctly or incorrectly. The designers, however, developed a true/false format that they hoped would be more interesting to those taking the test and at the same time yield more information than a standard true/false test. For each question, students could answer that they were "reasonably sure" of a true or false answer, or that they were "not sure but probably" the answer was true or false, or that they didn't know the answer. That way, the tests measured not only what students knew but also their confidence in that knowledge.

Administration and Scoring

Before presenting the tests, instructors gathered data on student demographics, such as intracompany organization, occupation, time in profession, and time in company. That data would be used, for example, to analyze which internal organizations did particularly good jobs of preparing their students.

Students took the pre-tests before taking the course and the post-tests several days after it. The tests were administered on optical mark-read forms, and the programs that computed the responses were designed to score the tests in several different ways, to take advantage of the unique test format. Descriptions of the scores follow.

S1

First, each test was scored according to "reasonably sure" responses only. That score (S1) represented the test's primary score and was the first one the students received as part of their feedback. One may argue that S1 results underestimate the true score, because guesses (those answers in the "not sure" category) are not included in its computation. The logic was that because the subject matter was critical to a student's job, being unsure about a principle or fact did not meet the criterion of knowing. In any case, results showed that the following, more lenient computation might have served as the primary test score without altering conclusions.

S2

The second method of scoring the tests was to measure both "sure" and "not sure" answers; in that manner, S2 resembled traditional test scoring, where guessing is included. For anyone who gets at least one correct "not sure" answer, S2 will be higher, obviously, than S1.

C1

The confidence index represented the percentage of answers that the students felt "sure" about — the higher the percentage of "sure" answers, the greater confidence the student indicated. A 100 percent C1, for example, meant that the student was sure about all of his or her responses. On the other hand, the score did not reflect the actual correctness of those responses.

IS

The intuitive score was the percentage of correct answers in the category of "not sure." IS was used only for pre-test data, because students generally use intuition, rather than knowledge, prior to learning; IS answered the question, "Are the students guessing correctly?" The "don't know" category served as an overflow — in order to keep the "not sure" category unaffected, it did not enter into the computation. In fact, the "don't know" category was rarely used by the students. For reasons of interpretability and reliability, an IS was not computed for a student if he or she provided fewer than three "not sure" responses.

Gain

Gain is the difference between the pre-test S1 and post-test S1.

Reaction

At the end of the test, the students rated their overall satisfaction with the course on a scale of one (high) to five (low).

Means and Correlations

Figure 14.1 shows the means and standard deviations for the four variables in the experimental testing. As expected, S2 showed a higher mean value than S1. That difference is more pronounced in pre- than in post-test data, probably because only a small percentage of answers were "not sure" on the post-test, as the higher post-test CI reflects. One can note in passing that the training had a strong effect on each variable.

Figure 14.1. Means and Standard Deviations
for Different Scoring Methods

	Mean	SD
Pre-test		
S1 (score on "reasonably sure" answers only)	52.9	17.4
S2 (score on "reasonably sure" and "not sure" answers)	70.8	10.7
CI (confidence index)	65.4	21.6
IS (intuitive score—correct answers marked "not sure")	55.2	29.6
Post-test		
S1	79.9	9.9
S2	82.9	8.7
CI	94.4	8.2
Gain (difference between pre-test and post-test S1)	27.4	18.4
Reaction (students' overall satisfaction: 1 = high; 5 = low)	1.5	.7

Note: Sample sizes for pre-test varibles, 2,210; for post-test variables, 2,226; for gain, 1,812; and for reaction, 1,511. Intuitive score was not calculated for post-test.

Figure 14.2. Percentage Correct of
Answers Marked "Reasonably Sure"

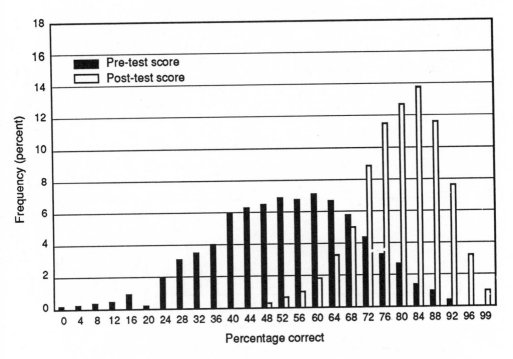

Figures 14.2 and 14.3 illustrate the relationship between S1 and CI across the range of students. In both sets of scores, increases in means and decreases in variances occurred between the tests, but one can see that the shape of the distributions differs from one to the other, CI piling up at the 100-percent ceiling.

Figure 14.4 shows the correlations between the pre- and post-test variables. The strongest relationships are between S1 and C1 for pre-test data, which indicates that the surer the students were about their answers, the higher their scores were.

On the post-test, the correlation drops to .58, due to the decreased standard deviation (see Figure 14.1). Strong negative correlations between both pre-test S1 and CI and the gain highlight the fact that lower scores in correctness and confidence on the pre-test meant greater increases in post-test knowledge; that slant toward low initial scores is a typical problem of gain scores.

Figure 14.3. Percentage Correct of Answers Marked "Reasonably Sure"

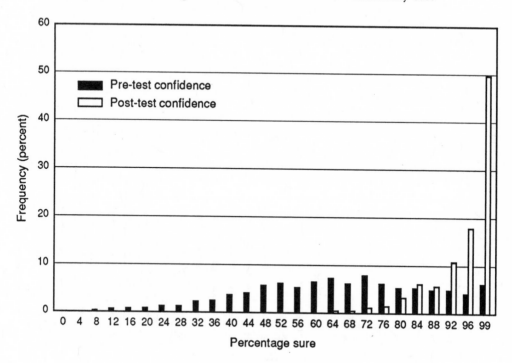

Figure 14.4. Major Variable Intercorrelations

		Pre-test				Post-test				
		S1	*S2*	*CI*	*IS*	*S1*	*S2*	*CI*	*Gain*	*Reaction*
Pre-test	S1		.58	.92	−.44	.19	.03	.31	−.85	.02
	S2			.36	.13	.21	.18	.12	−.44	.01
	CI				−.48	.13	−.05	.34	−.81	.02
	IS					.00	.10	−.15	.41	.00
Post-test	S1						.84	.58	.36	−.02
	S2							.13	.43	−.01
	CI								−.02	−.02
	Gain									−.03

Note: Sample sizes for the above correlations vary from 1,511 to 1,259. However, only underlined correlations are not significant at at least the *p* < .05 level.

The correlation between S1 and S2 on the pre-test was only .58, indicating the distinction between the two types of scoring. On the post-test, the scores correlate strongly, due to fewer "not sure" responses.

It is interesting to note that reaction had a correlation of virtually zero with measures of pre- or post-knowledge (.02 and − .02 respectively) and knowledge gain (− .03). Although those low correlations may be due in part to the restricted range of the generally favorable reaction ratings, they also reflect the probability that course ratings and actual learning are different measurements. That distinction may have implications for the use of Kirkpatrick's Step One (reaction) measures to assess the impact of training programs.

Using the Results

The indices obtained from the tests aided the organization in several ways:

- Course administrators analyzed each question and used the results to help redesign the course.
- A larger study used the results to measure course effectiveness.
- The demographic analysis of the results aided in an organizational examination.
- The measurement results served to rate the effectiveness of the course instructors.

In the step that took most advantage of the new test format, students received feedback on the results. Figure 14.5 shows a fictional example of typical feedback to a student. The form, generated entirely by computer, was accompanied by a cover letter that explained the nature of the various scores.

Discussion

The introduction of the CI, or confidence index, as reflected in the CI data and indirectly through the other scores, may be the

Figure 14.5. Student Feedback Form

Personal and Confidential
Course Score Card

A

Report Date 4-12-89   Organization: Marketing
Class Number: 554a   Function: Administration
Name: John Q. Student
Years in Company: 5   Avg. Years in Company: 9.4
Months in Job: 1   Avg. Years in Position: 2.1

B

Score (%)

	Your Score	*All Marketing*	*All Administration*	*All Students*
Pre-test	28	47	47	47
Post-test	72	79	76	80

C

Confidence Index (%)

	Your Score	*All Marketing*	*All Administration*	*All Students*
Pre-test	40	61	59	58
Post-test	88	96	91	94

D

Intuitive Score (%)

	Your Score	*Number Answered "Not Sure"*	*All Marketing*	*All Administration*	*All Students*
Pre-test	67	12	54	55	57

---

biggest success of the test format. Behavior in the workplace is probably a function not only of what a student knows but also of how certain he or she is of that knowledge. Moreover, the fact that students did not have problems understanding the format could indicate that separating knowing into "sure" and "not sure" is a practical measurement approach.

Further research in the design of the questions is certainly possible. For example, a multiple-choice test format could present questions and options followed by a secondary scale on which the student could indicate his or her level of confidence. Of course, the most interesting aspect of the test format would be a validation that related scores to performance: does the level of confidence add to the prediction of performance supplied by the standard, unitary measurement of knowledge?

This method of testing measures knowledge and confidence simultaneously; to put it another way, it provides a way to take the guessing out of testing. The test format and its results can be interpreted easily, and many students expressed appreciation for the feedback they received. In industrial training and development, few methods can accurately measure knowledge gain and retention—perhaps IBM's experimental measurement method could be valuable for other companies as well.

Chapter 15

Evaluating a Training Program on Presentation Skills

A t Arthur Andersen & Co., presentation skills are considered to be very important. To meet the need, a training program was developed and offered to those who could benefit from it. Evaluation was done at levels 2 and 3 to measure the effectiveness of the program. Pretests and posttests were used to determine whether the course resulted in persistent changes in knowledge, skills, and attitudes and the extent to which changes in behavior occurred. The evaluation services group developed a sophisticated design for the Management Development Department to use in evaluating the program.

Arthur Andersen & Company

Steven Bond, Manager, Center for Professional Education
Arthur Andersen & Co., St. Charles, Illinois

The Context

The Centers for Professional Education

Arthur Andersen and Andersen Consulting are professional services providers that make up the Arthur Andersen Worldwide Organization. Arthur Andersen provides auditing, business advisory services, and tax consultation, and Andersen Consulting offers business integration and information systems to clients around the world. At its centers for professional education in St. Charles, Illinois, and Veldhoven, The Netherlands, more than 260 education professionals comprising the Professional Education Division design and develop training programs offered to Andersen's 60,000 employees at training sites and offices around the world. The 6,000,000 hours of training delivered annually cover technical areas, business strategy, and management and leadership development.

Management Development

Traditionally, the Arthur Andersen Worldwide Organization has promoted people from within the organization to management levels. Therefore, it has a tradition of management development programming that includes training, job assignment, and other personal development experiences. The management development training group provides a wide variety of personal, professional, and interpersonal programs as part of this overall development process. These programs are based on needs assessment findings and are evaluated formatively throughout the development process. Occasional summative evaluations are also completed.

Evaluation Services

Beginning in 1979, the centers for professional development have used an independent evaluation function separate from the training development groups. This function provides a variety of services ranging from survey research and needs assessment to follow-up studies for program evaluation. The specialists in this evaluation group work cooperatively with the training development teams to ensure quality in the training programs and to provide decision makers with accurate, timely information.

This report summarizes a follow-up evaluation of a course on effective presentations conducted by the evaluation services group for Management Development.

The Course

In a professional services relationship, where confidence in an individual is often the determining factor in obtaining and retaining a client, it is important for the service provider not only to exhibit deep technical competence but also to inspire interpersonal confidence. An ability to make oral presentations in a self-assured, professional manner is a part of projecting an image of poise and self-control to the client.

The two-day effective presentations course, which has a maximum class size of sixteen participants, is offered approximately 120 times per year. Instructor-led periods are followed by sessions in which participants have opportunities to practice the skills presented in lecture. Participants give six presentations. Each is videotaped and critiqued by fellow participants and instructors. The objectives of the course are to help to improve the participants' eye contact; vocal projection; stance, gestures and animation; and use of visuals, silence, and pauses and to help them organize effectively what they say.

The Evaluation

Purpose and Overall Design

The purpose of the summative evaluation of the effective presentations course was to determine whether the course resulted in persistent changes in participants' knowledge, behaviors, or attitudes related to the making of presentations. The focus of the evaluation was to assess participants' behavior while actually making presentations, to determine whether participants' self-assessment changed during the course, and to assess whether participants retained changes in knowledge, attitudes, and behaviors over time. A pre-post follow-up within-subjects design was used. This design had the following structure:

Measure —— Train —— Measure —— Wait —— Measure

Information was obtained from participants on three occasions: at the beginning of the course, at the end of the course, and after the course. On each occasion, participants completed a questionnaire and were videotaped while making a presentation.

Data Collection Process

Information was collected at four different sessions of the course. These sessions were selected not at random but because they were scheduled within the time frame of the study. During each session, an evaluator observed the instruction, administered questionnaires before and after the training to each participant, ensured that the videotapings were completed correctly and retained, conducted informal interviews with participants, and provided information to participants about the follow-up phase of the evaluation. Beginning six months after the first session, follow-up questionnaires were distributed, and arrangements were made to complete follow-up videotapings with participants from five U.S. and four European offices. The time that elapsed between completion of the course and follow-up taping ranged from about one to eight months.

Questionnaires

The three questionnaires included items that obtained participants' self-assessments in the following areas: demographics; training and experience related to the making of presentations; self-ratings on general presentation skills; self-reported confidence in making presentations; and performance in specific areas, such as eye contact, gestures, voice projection, stance and posture, use of visuals, question-and-answer sessions, and organization of content. To avoid introducing participants to specific course content before the course began, some questions were not asked on the questionnaire administered before training.

Videotaping

Each participant included in the final behavioral analysis was videotaped before and after training and at the follow-up session.

Before Training. The first presentation made by participants in the course served as the pre-measure. Participants had been presented with no course content at the time when they made this presentation. In the event that this first presentation was too short to obtain an adequate sample of behavior, the first portion of the second presentation was used to assess the skills for which a participant had not yet received instruction.

After Training. The last (sixth) presentation in the course served as the post measure. At that point, participants had received all course content. However, they did receive feedback on the presentation subsequent to taping.

Follow-up Session. Arrangements were made with participants to prepare and deliver a five-to-ten minute presentation in their office. These presentations were either presentations to other office employees, or they were practice for upcoming client presentations. Most of these presentations were attended by either a Management Development or an evaluation services staff person, who videotaped the session.

Behavioral Rating System

A coding structure and observation checklist were created for analysis of the videotaped presentations. The structure was based on two considerations: course content and ability to measure differences in performance in a videotaped presentation. The rating system had six general categories: head movement and eye contact, gestures and upper body movement, lower body movement and stance, voice quality, organization of content, and overall presentation. Each category represents the translation of a major area of course content into a set of specific behavioral measures.

The frequency of behaviors in the first four categories were recorded during four fifteen-second periods for a total of one minute for each. The presentation was then replayed, and raters recorded information and assigned ratings for voice projection and speed (subcategories of the voice quality category), organization of content, and overall presentation.

Four raters were trained to use the behavioral rating system. Two raters simultaneously viewed and coded each videotaped presentation. Raters were rotated so that three of the four individuals rated tapes with at least two other raters. Tapes were rated in random order. Interrater reliabilities were computed across each pair of raters and across the behavioral categories. The lowest reliabilities were in the more subjective areas, such as voice quality, but overall the intercorrelations were modest to strong, with about half being above .80 and more than two-thirds above .60.

Use of visuals and question-and-answer sessions were excluded from the behavioral rating system because participants did not have an opportunity to demonstrate these skills on all presentations. The next six sections describe the categories rated.

Head Movement and Eye Contact. It was not possible to discern the duration of participants' eye contact accurately while observing the taped presentations. Therefore, shifts in head movement were used instead. (Individuals often break eye contact without shifting their head, but they are not likely to shift their head while retaining eye contact with a specific individual. If an individual made three head shifts in a fifteen-second period, it was assumed that eye contact was being held for an average of five seconds. If fifteen shifts occurred, the average duration of eye contact was calculated to have been one second.) This is a conservative measure that gives participants credit for more effective eye contact than was likely to have occurred.

Two types of behavior were recorded. The first was the number of head shifts, and the second was the number of glances directed at something other than the audience, such as the ceiling, floor, or walls (ineffective behavior).

Gestures and Upper Body Movement. Three subcategories were established that subsumed the majority of possible behaviors likely to be seen. Participants were rated as gesturing effectively (moving one or both hands above elbow height), assuming a "parade rest" stance (with arms and hands relaxed at sides), or doing something ineffective (for example, holding their hands in fig leaf or praying positions, holding onto a flipchart or podium, or making small, low gestures).

Lower Body Movement and Stance. Three subcategories were used. Participants were assessed as standing appropriately (feet stationary and shoulder-width apart, weight evenly distributed), moving with purpose, or doing something ineffective (weight unevenly distributed, pacing, rocking, or standing turned toward the flip-chart or overhead screen).

Voice. Three subcategories were used. Nonwords (*umh*'s, *ahh*'s, fillers, words or sentences restarted) were counted. Voice projection (strong/loud, acceptable, or too soft) and speed (too fast, appropriate, or too slow) were rated at the end of the taped presentation.

Organization of Content. The introduction, body, and conclusion of each presentation were rated as present/effective, acceptable, or weak/absent.

Overall Presentation. Ratings were assigned to the overall presentation on a scale ranging from 1 (very poor) to 5 (very good). Pluses and minuses could also be assigned. This resulted in a fourteen-point scale ranging from 1 to 5 + .

Participant Sample

Data on performance before and after training were obtained from forty-six participants in the four sessions. Follow-up questionnaires were distributed to all participants with the exception of four individuals who had left the firm or who had taken the course in preparation to be certified to teach it. The follow-up questionnaire was completed by thirty participants (71 percent). Follow-up videotapes were obtained from nineteen participants. These nineteen individuals were from nine offices; six of them were from European offices. Follow-up questionnaires were received from eighteen of the nineteen individuals for whom there were follow-up tapes. The data analyses were based on the data available from this group of nineteen participants. Key characteristics of this group (years with the firm, experience and training related to the making of presentations, and self-assessment of overall presentation ability) were compared with the characteristics of participants for whom the data were incomplete. No significant differences were found. Therefore, conclusions based on the sample of nineteen individuals appeared to be generalizable.

Participants' performances during videotaped presentations and their responses on questionnaires were analyzed to determine the changes that had occurred. To assess whether any changes in participants' behavior or questionnaire responses were statistically significant, the evaluators used t-tests (paired comparison). Comparisons were completed for each of the categories identified in the preceding section.

Performing numerous t-tests increases the probability that chance differences due to sampling error rather than to the effect of the training will occur. To control for this, the criterion for concluding that differences were statistically significant was made more strict than it would have been used if fewer comparisons had been made. Use of a strict criterion (.01) for individual comparisons increased the confidence with which conclusions about the effects of the course in numerous specific areas could be made.

The Findings

General Findings

Results of the analysis on each of the categories for which questionnaire and behavioral data were collected were summarized. Mean responses on the pre, post, and follow-up questionnaires and results of the related significance tests were calculated, and information about the frequency and effectiveness of specific behaviors during the videotaped pre, post, and follow-up presentations was provided.

Overall, participants' self-assessments significantly improved in all areas included on the questionnaires. Participants' actual behaviors while making presentations improved in several areas, including overall effectiveness, gestures and upper body movement, stationary feet, voice projection, avoiding nonwords, and providing an effective conclusion. Improved performance levels were retained from the post to follow-up presentations in each of these areas with the exception of effectiveness in delivering conclusions (a part of organization of content).

A Word About Self-Reported
Reaction Data on Overall Effectiveness

Participants' self-assessments of their overall presentation ability improved significantly. Self-assessment of their overall presentation ability did not change between the time immediately after training and follow-up.

Raters' assessments of participants' overall effectiveness while making the videotaped presentations concurred with participants' self-assessments. There was a significant improvement in the overall ratings of the presentations at the end of the course over ratings at the beginning of the course. There was no significant change in participants' overall effectiveness between the end of training and the follow-up presentations, which suggests that the improvements made during the course were retained over time. These quantitative results parallel participants' verbal comments offered during and after the course.

Concluding Comments

The study just described was designed to be a rigorous look at retention of learned behaviors and application of those behaviors in a nontraining setting. While the follow-up sessions were not training per se, they were not fully real-world applications either. This reflects a constraint in practice. It is sometimes simply not feasible to follow the trainee into his or her workplace in order to measure the trainee's performance. Significant impact questions are left unanswered by this type of research. Do changed presentation skills make a difference in a person's professional relationship–building capability? Do superior presentation skills translate into reduced cost and/or increased revenue and therefore greater long-run profits? Before these questions of impact can be addressed realistically, two fundamental questions must be answered: Did the training result in a behavioral change? And did the change persist? This evaluation is an example of one step in the overall evaluation process that should accompany training designed to affect organizational performance.

Chapter 16

Evaluating a Training Program for District Managers

In this case study, a new measuring instrument is developed to evaluate a training program designed to improve the behavior of district managers. This instrument, called the *gap analysis checklist*, is completed by the immediate supervisor of a participant to measure the extent of the change in behavior that results from the training program.

A Large Automotive Company

Jane Holcomb, On-Target Training
Playa del Rey, California

Introduction

In the company where this case study took place, district managers (DMs) act as liaison between the corporation and the automotive dealers who sell cars. The study included district sales managers, district parts managers, and district service managers.

District sales managers help dealers sell cars. They train salesmen, help dealers with marketing plans, provide advertising advice, plan promotions, and offer other help in selling cars.

District parts managers help dealers with inventory and handle distribution of parts to customers, auto body shops, and others who want to buy parts from the manufacturer.

District service managers help service departments to become a profit center by assisting with the training of technicians (formerly called *mechanics*) and providing advice and help as needed.

Many of the DMs are young, bright kids recruited directly from colleges and universities. They typically are ambitious and single, and they do not object to spending many hours on the road visiting dealers. They see the job as secure and sexy and as providing status. They like the new car that is provided to them. Most of their training is on the job, provided by their immediate supervisor, the regional manager (RM).

The DMs face several problems. Some dealers perceive them as kids who are still wet behind the ears and in no position to tell them how to run their business. Dealers are an independent breed, and DMs need excellent interpersonal skills to enforce corporate policy with dealers. The three DMs each work with a separate dealer function, and the right hand often does not know what the left hand is doing.

The Training Program

The two-week training program was designed to develop teamwork among the three DMs, to improve their attitude and knowledge about dealers and how they can give them the most help, and to improve communications skills.

Twenty-five district managers from across the country were brought in at a time to attend the intensive two-week training program. It was conducted by training professionals under the leadership of a guru who was well known and respected in the automotive industry. He designed the program and selected the leaders to conduct it. Developed and implemented at great expense, it included videos and other aids, including a manual the size of a large city telephone directory. The program was held at a first-class hotel, where the DMs were housed and fed like kings for the entire program.

Program content touched on many subjects, including consultive selling skills, communications, time management, marketing techniques, customer service, and basics of finance. The content was based on what DMs wanted and needed to know to do their job effectively.

The Evaluation

The evaluation was designed to measure change in behavior. The corporate operational training manager wanted to develop a team of DMs under the leadership of a well-known expert. He wanted the program to be high class and high tech. He wanted the evaluation to be done by a third party to determine the extent to which the DMs applied the attitudes, knowledge, and skills taught in the program.

The Evaluation Plan

The evaluation plan had six steps:

1. Design a program to meet the needs of the DMs.
2. Design an evaluation instrument to measure changes in behavior.
3. Train the immediate supervisors of the participants—the regional managers—to do the evaluation.
4. Collect, tabulate, and analyze the completed evaluations.
5. Feed the evaluation results back to the regional managers.
6. Use the evaluations and suggestions received from the regional managers to formulate suggestions for program redesign.

The Evaluation Design

A form called the *gap analysis checklist* was developed. Exhibit 16.1 shows sample items from this form. Items were based on the objectives and content of the training program. The evaluation sought to measure the extent to which the DMs were applying the content of the program. Regional managers were to use the form when the DMs returned from training.

Exhibit 16.1. Sample Items from the Gap Analysis Checklist

1. Ability to assist dealers to achieve good CSI performance in the dealerships

Can your DMs do the following?

	Yes	Needs improvement
Analyze and prioritize customer satisfaction information?		
Encourage dealers to post results?		
Encourage dealers to convey corporate guidelines on customer service for dealership employees?		
Help dealers to design a compensation plan for employees tied to customer satisfaction results?		
Discuss customer satisfaction information in regular department manager meetings?		
Recommend customer relations training for appropriate dealership employees?		
Close a consumer affairs report on the datanet system and teach dealers how to use the system?		
Advise and counsel dealers with low customer satisfaction scores?		
Develop an action plan to improve?		
Follow up on the action plan to see that the commitment is carried out?		

2. Analyze and evaluate dealership performance using financial statements and develop corrective action

Can your DMs do the following?

	Yes	Needs improvement
Explain key elements to you before making a dealer contact?		
Mention positive results as well as areas needing attention?		
Recognize and understand each dealer's cash flow problems?		
Make appropriate recommendations for improvement?		
Discuss trends in composite group, district, and region?		
Is the district manager sensitive to the need for confidentiality?		
Use financial statements and expense guidelines as a basis for financial discussions?		
Is the district manager able to evaluate department productivity using basic training worksheets?		
Identify financial red flags and help to devise action plans?		
Follow up on previous financial action plan items?		

When the training program was completed, the regional managers were walked through the program so that they would understand its objectives and content. They were given a copy of the manual that each participant had received. The gap analysis checklist was introduced, and they were instructed in how to use it. When they returned to their territory, they were told to ride with each DM and complete the form. Besides evaluating attitude, knowledge, and behavior, they were asked to coach the DM to correct any errors and reinforce what he had learned in the program.

One unexpected outcome of the evaluation was a loud outcry from the regional managers concerning the program itself. They were upset that they had not been involved in the development of the program. Needless to say, their comments and suggestions were considered when the program was revised. Not only did their input make the program more practical, but it also improved their support of the program and their cooperation in regard to the evaluation.

Results of the Evaluation

Approximately 35 percent of the regional managers completed the gap analysis checklist and returned it to the operations manager. Those who did not complete the checklist gave such excuses as these:

"I don't have time to ride with the district managers."
"Evaluating training isn't part of my job."
"I had no part in planning the program, and I don't agree with what was taught."

Those who did use the checklist felt that it was a useful tool for helping them to develop their district managers.

Recommendations

Based on the experiences described in this case study, the following principles should be the basis for future programs:

1. It is important to get input from the immediate supervisors before deciding on the training content and the methods for evaluating its effectiveness.
2. The evaluation of training should be included in the job description of supervisors so they consider it to be part of their job.
3. In order for this kind of evaluation to be effective, the organization must be stable. During this evaluation, the company reorganized, and many regional managers were transferred to other districts.

Chapter 17

Evaluating a Training Program on Developing Supervisory Skills

This research study designed to measure changes in behavior and results evaluated a three-day institute that was held in Milwaukee. A similar program is offered in both Madison and Milwaukee approximately fifteen times a year.

Management Institute, University of Wisconsin

Donald L. Kirkpatrick, Professor Emeritus
University of Wisconsin, Milwaukee

Developing Supervisory Skills, a three-day institute conducted by the University of Wisconsin Management Institute, included six three-hour sessions on the following topics: giving orders, training, appraising employee performance, preventing and handling grievances, making decisions, and initiating change. All the leaders were staff members of the University of Wisconsin Management Institute. Teaching methods included lecture, guided discussion, "buzz" groups, role playing, case studies, supervisory inventories, and films and other visual aids.

Research Design

Each participant completed a questionnaire at the start of the program. Interviews of each participant were conducted at his or her workplace between two and three months after the conclusion of the program. On the same visit, the participant's immediate supervisor was also interviewed. Out of a total enrollment of fifty-seven participants, data were obtained from forty-three and from their bosses, and those data are included in this study. Exhibit 17.1 shows the findings on demographics and general issues.

Research Results

In this situation, it was not possible to measure on a before-and-after basis. Instead, interviews were used to determine how behavior and results after the program compared with behavior before the program. Both the participant and his or her immediate supervisor were interviewed, and their responses were compared.

The first part of each interview determined overall changes in behavior and results. Exhibit 17.2 shows the responses. The second part of the interview determined changes related to each of the six topics discussed in the program. The reader should note that all responses in Exhibit 17.2 and Tables 17.1 through 17.8 are given in percentages. When two figures are given, the first is the percentage response from participants, and the second is the percentage response from their immediate supervisors.

One question asked, on an overall basis, To what extent has the participant's job behavior changed since the program? Table 17.1 shows the responses in regard to changes in performance and attitude. Positive changes were indicated in all nine areas, with the greatest improvement occurring in attitudes.

To the question, What results have occurred since the program? Table 17.2 shows the responses from participants and immediate supervisors. Positive results were observed in all eight categories. In four areas, one or two supervisors observed negative results. And one participant (2 percent) indicated that employee attitudes and morale were somewhat worse.

It is interesting to note that, in nearly all cases, participants were more likely than supervisors to indicate that positive changes

Exhibit 17.1. Questionnaire Responses: Demographics

---

1. Describe your organization:
   a. Size
      - (4) less than 100 employees
      - (10) 100–500 employees
      - (3) 500–1,000 employees
      - (26) more than 1,000 employees
   b. Products
      - (15) consumer
      - (11) industrial
      - (12) both
      - (5) other
2. Describe yourself:
   a. Title
      - (33) foreman or supervisor
      - (10) general foreman or superintendent
   b. How many people do you supervise?
      - (1) 0–5
      - (9) 6–10
      - (6) 11–15
      - (8) 16–20
      - (19) more than 20
   c. Whom do you supervise?
      - (26) all men
      - (11) mostly men
      - (6) mostly women
   d. What kind of workers do you supervise?
      - (14) production, unskilled
      - (23) production, semiskilled
      - (12) production, skilled
      - (2) maintenance
      - (9) office
   e. Before attending the program, how much were you told about it?
      - (3) complete information
      - (8) quite a lot
      - (20) a little
      - (12) practically nothing
   f. To what extent do you feel that you will be able to improve your supervisory performance by attending this program?
      - (21) to a large extent
      - (22) to some extent
      - (0) very little
3. How would you describe your top management?
      - (31) liberal (encourages change and suggestions)
      - (9) middle-of-the-road
      - (3) conservative (discourages change and suggestions)
4. How would you describe your immediate supervisor?
      - (35) liberal

Exhibit 17.1. Questionnaire Responses: Demographics *(continued)*

---

    (8) middle-of-the-road
    (0) conservative

5. How often does your supervisor ask you for ideas to solve departmental problems?
    (19) frequently
    (19) sometimes
    (5) hardly ever

6. To what extent will your supervisor encourage you to apply the ideas and techniques you learned in this program?
    (14) to a large extent
    (14) to some extent
    (1) very little
    (14) not sure

Exhibit 17.2. Questionnaire Responses: Behavior Changes

---

1. To what extent has the program improved the working relationship between the participant and his or her immediate supervisor?
    (23, 12) to a large extent
    (51, 32) to some extent
    (26, 56) no change
    (0, 0) made it worse

2. Since the program, how much two-way communciation has taken place between the participant and his or her immediate supervisor?
    (12, 5) much more
    (63, 46) some more
    (25, 49) no change
    (0, 0) some less
    (0, 0) much less

3. Since the program, how much interest has the participant taken in his or her subordinates?
    (26, 5) much more
    (67, 49) some more
    (7, 46) no change
    (0, 0) some less
    (0, 0) much less

Table 17.1. Change in Behavior

Supervisory Areas	Much Better	Somewhat Better	No Change	Somewhat Worse	Much Worse	Don't Know
Giving Orders	25, 12	70, 65	5, 14	0, 0	0, 0	0, 9
Training	22, 17	56, 39	22, 39	0, 0	0, 0	0, 5
Making Decisions	35, 14	58, 58	7, 23	0, 0	0, 0	0, 5
Initiating Change	21, 9	53, 53	26, 30	0, 0	0, 0	0, 7
Appraising Employee Performance	21, 7	50, 42	28, 36	0, 0	0, 0	0, 12
Preventing and Handling Grievances	12, 7	42, 40	46, 46	0, 0	0, 0	0, 7
Attitude Toward Job	37, 23	37, 53	26, 23	0, 0	0, 0	0, 0
Attitude Toward Subordinates	40, 7	42, 60	19, 30	0, 0	0, 0	0, 2
Attitude Toward Management	42, 26	26, 35	32, 37	0, 0	0, 0	0, 2

Table 17.2. Results

Performance Benchmarks	Much Better	Somewhat Better	No Change	Somewhat Worse	Much Worse	Don't Know
Quantity of Production	5, 5	43, 38	50, 50	0, 2	0, 0	0, 5
Quality of Production	10, 7	60, 38	28, 52	0, 0	0, 0	0, 2
Safety	21, 7	28, 37	49, 56	0, 0	0, 0	0, 0
Housekeeping	23, 14	32, 35	42, 46	0, 5	0, 0	0, 0
Employee Attitudes and Morale	12, 7	56, 53	28, 32	2, 5	0, 0	0, 2
Employee Attendance	7, 2	23, 19	67, 77	0, 0	0, 0	0, 0
Employee Promptness	7, 2	32, 16	58, 81	0, 0	0, 0	0, 0
Employee Turnover	5, 0	14, 16	79, 79	0, 5	0, 0	0, 0

had taken place. There is no way of telling who is right. The important fact is that both participants and supervisors saw positive changes in both behavior and results.

Tables 17.3 to 17.8 show the responses to the questions asked on each of the six topics that the program covered. The responses are uniformly positive.

Summary and Conclusions

Because this program is repeated a number of times a year, it was worthwhile to spend the time and money that it takes to do a detailed evaluation. It was rewarding to find such positive responses from both the participants and their immediate supervisors. Because it was not possible to measure behavior and results on a before-and-after basis, the evaluation design took the alternative approach: to determine how behavior and results after the program differed from what they had been before the program.

The important thing for the reader of this case study is not what the researchers found out as a result of the research but what they did. You can borrow the design and approach and use it as is or modify it to meet your own situation. For example, you may want to add another set of interviews with subordinates of the participant and/or others who are in a position to observe the behavior of participants. You may even want to use a control group to eliminate other factors that could have caused changes in either behavior or results. In any case, consider evaluating in terms of behavior and even results, especially if the program is going to be repeated a number of times in the future.

Table 17.3. Giving Orders

	Much More	Somewhat More	No Change	Somewhat Less	Much Less	Don't Know
Since the program, is the participant taking more time to plan his orders?	17, 23	58, 60	16, 12	9, 0	0, 0	0, 5
Since the program, is the participant taking more time to prepare the order receiver?	24, 17	71, 57	5, 19	0, 0	0, 0	0, 7
Since the program, is the participant getting more voluntary cooperation from his employees?	26, 0	37, 56	37, 23	0, 0	0, 0	0, 21
Since the program, is the participant doing more in the way of making sure the order receiver understands the order?	51, 21	44, 44	5, 7	0, 0	0, 0	0, 28
Since the program, is the participant taking more time to make sure the order receiver is following instructions?	21, 16	60, 58	19, 12	0, 0	0, 0	0, 14
Since the program, is the participant making more of an effort to praise his employees for a job well done?	24, 30	50, 22	8, 7	0, 0	0, 0	0, 41
Since the program, is the participant doing more follow-up to see that his orders were properly carried out?	37, 21	39, 42	24, 26	0, 0	0, 0	0, 11

Table 17.4. Training Employees

Questions	Yes / Participant Always / Does Not Apply	Much More	No / Participant Usually / Somewhat More	Not Sure / No Change	Participant Sometimes / Somewhat Less	Much Less	No New or Transferred Employees — Participant Never / Don't Know
Since the participant attended the program, are his new or transferred employees better trained?	63, 46		9, 0	23, 43			6, 11
Before the program, who trained the workers?	16, 13		42, 45		34, 31		8, 11
Since the program, who trained the workers?	15, 18		45, 42		32, 29		8, 11
Since the program, if someone else trains the employees, has the participant become more observant and taken a more active interest in the training process?	14, 11	22, 16	40, 27	24, 30	0, 0	0, 0	0, 16
Since the program, if the participant trains the employees, is he making more of an effort in seeing that the employees are well trained?	8, 5	42, 24	42, 42	8, 18	0, 0	0, 0	0, 11
Since the program, is the participant more inclined to be patient while training?	8, 11	24, 5	47, 50	21, 20	0, 3	0, 0	0, 11
Since the program, while teaching an operation, is the participant asking for more questions to ensure understanding?	8, 21	27, 14	46, 46	9, 8	0, 0	0, 0	0, 11
Since the program, is the participant better prepared to teach?	8, 11	29, 18	47, 52	16, 8	0, 0	0, 0	0, 11
Since the program, is the participant doing more follow-up to check the trainees' progress?	0, 0	41, 21	38, 49	21, 14	0, 0	0, 0	0, 16

Table 17.5. Appraising Employees' Performance

	Yes	No
Is the participant required to complete appraisal forms on his subordinates?	62, 69	38, 31

	Does Not Apply	Large Extent	Some Extent	Little	Don't Know
Before the program, if the participant conducted appraisal interviews, to what extent did he emphasize past performance?	48, 40	10, 5	40, 12	2, 14	0, 29
Before the program, to what extent did the participant try to determine the goals and objectives of his employees?	—	5, 15	65, 52	30, 30	0, 3
Before the program, to what extent did the participant praise the work of his employees?	—	8, 12	77, 52	15, 18	0, 18

	Does Not Apply	Much More	Somewhat More	No Change	Somewhat Less	Much Less	Don't Know
Since the program, is the participant doing more follow-up to see that the objectives of the appraisal interview are being carried out?	48, 40	10, 5	24, 21	14, 19	2, 0	0, 0	0, 14
Since the program, during an appraisal interview, is the participant placing more emphasis on future performance?	48, 40	24, 7	17, 10	10, 14	0, 2	0, 0	0, 26
Since the program, is the participant making more of an effort to determine the goals and objectives of his employees?	—	22, 15	60, 50	18, 18	0, 0	0, 0	0, 18
Since the program, how much does the participant praise his employees?	—	22, 10	40, 38	38, 38	0, 2	0, 0	0, 12

Table 17.6. Preventing and Handling Grievances

	Yes	No
Do participant's employees belong to a union?	69, 69	31, 31

	Always Defended Management / *Much More*	*Usually Defended Management* / *Somewhat More*	*Participant Always* / *Acted Objectively* / *No Change*	*Participant Usually* / *Usually Defended Employees* / *Somewhat Less*	*Much Less*	*Participant Sometimes* / *Always Defended Employees* / *No Union*	*Participant Never* / *Don't Know*
Before the program, if an employee had a grievance, who usually settled it?			10, 12	64, 38		24, 43	2, 5
Since the program, who usually settles employee grievances?			10, 12	69, 48		21, 38	0, 2
Before the program, to what extent did the participant defend management versus the employees in regard to grievance problems?	34, 17	22, 39	44, 20	0, 10		0, 0	0, 15
Since the program, is the participant more inclined to the management viewpoint regarding grievances and complaints?	19, 14	31, 29	48, 48	2, 0	0, 0		0, 9
Since the program, has there been a change in the number of grievances in the participant's department?	2, 5	7, 14	81, 71	10, 5	0, 0		0, 5
Since the program, has the degree of seriousness of grievances changed?	0, 0	2, 2	74, 74	24, 12	0, 7		0, 5
Since the program, has the participant been better able to satisfy employee complaints before they reach the grievance stage?	17, 7	31, 52	26, 24	0, 0	0, 2	26, 14	0, 5

Table 17.7. Making Decisions

	Yes	No	Don't Know
Participants only: Since the program, is the participant making better decisions?	88	2	10

	Much Better	Somewhat Better	No Change	Somewhat Worse	Much Worse	Don't Know
Supervisors only: Since the program, is the participant making better decisions?	12	68	10	0	0	10

	Frequently	Sometimes	Hardly Ever	Don't Know
Before the program, how often did the participant's boss involve or consult him in the decision-making process in the participant's department?	40, 65	45, 30	15, 5	
Before the program, to what extent did the participant involve or consult employees in the decision-making process?	24, 26	57, 38	19, 24	0, 10

Table 17.7. Making Decisions (continued)

	Much More	Somewhat More	No Change	Somewhat Less	Much Less	Don't Know
Since the program, how often does the participant's boss involve him in the departmental decision-making process?	13, 23	25, 17	60, 55	3, 3	0, 3	0, 0
Since the program, how often does the participant involve employees in the decision-making process?	26, 0	38, 43	33, 33	3, 7	0, 3	0, 14
Since the program, does the participant have less tendency to put off making decisions?	0, 0	0, 0	36, 33	36, 40	28, 22	0, 5
Since the program, is the participant holding more group meetings with employees?	12, 5	26, 17	62, 55	0, 0	0, 0	0, 24
Since the program, does the participant have more confidence in the decisions he makes?	29, 19	60, 60	12, 21	0, 0	0, 0	0, 0
Since the program, is the participant using a more planned approach to decision making (taking more time to define the problem and develop an answer)?	40, 14	50, 71	10, 7	0, 0	0, 0	0, 7
Since the program, does the participant take more time to evaluate the results of a decision?	24, 3	60, 62	14, 12	3, 0	0, 0	0, 24

Table 17.8. Initiating Change

	Frequently	Sometimes	Hardly Ever
Before the program, when the need for change arose, how often did the participant ask his subordinate for suggestions or ideas regarding the change or need for change?	21, 21	64, 52	14, 21
Before the program, how often did the participant inform his employees of the change and the reason for it?	50, 26	36, 55	14, 14

	Much More	Somewhat More	No Change	Somewhat Less	Much Less	Don't Know
Since the program, is the participant doing more follow-up to the change process to make sure it is going in the right direction?	38, 17	50, 60	12, 12	0, 0	0, 0	0, 12
Since the program, how often has the participant involved his subordinates by asking them for suggestions or ideas?	17, 2	43, 40	40, 38	0, 7	0, 0	0, 12
Since the program, is the participant doing more in the way of informing employees of impending change and the reasons for it?	33, 10	38, 45	29, 26	0, 2	0, 0	0, 17

Chapter 18

Evaluating a Sales Training Program

J.P. Huller was quoted at the beginning of Chapter 2 on the reasons for evaluating training programs. He stated that trainers must gain acceptance, trust, and respect by earning it. And the way to do it is by evaluating and reporting on the worth of training. That he practiced what he preached is demonstrated by this case study, which describes evaluation of a sales training program at level 4. The case includes J. P.'s philosophy of evaluation as well as a design for implementation that makes use of a control group.

Hobart Corporation

J. P. Huller, Senior Manager, Education and Training
Reynolds and Reynolds Computer Systems Division,
Dayton, Ohio
former Manager, Product Training Programs
Hobart Corporation, Troy, Ohio

Ellen B. Pullens, Project Leader, Product Training Programs
Hobart Corporation, Troy, Ohio

At Hobart, we found proof that training increased the profits of the organization. We found that training had a return on investment

(ROI) of 161 percent and that it had a potential of achieving 665 percent. Tables 18.1 and 18.2 come from our final report, which was used — successfully — to position the training function as a necessary part of the business.

This effort began when J. P. Huller sat in yet another national training conference listening to a session speaker tell him to prove that training pays and then show him a complex dissertation on the subject. Huller did not understand most of what was said and left feeling that it was simply too difficult for him to do.

The surprising truth is that it's not hard to prove that training pays. This very second, in meeting rooms around the world, managers are proving how their sales promotions, advertising, spiff program, or whatever paid off. They do it every day, and in most cases their programs, unlike training, did not have clear, measurable objectives.

After months of searching, we found that the only way to prove that training pays was right in front of us: *You must calculate payback, format your report, and present your results in exactly the same form in which your senior management receives all other payback reports.* The goal is to show that training programs are like any other business investment.

Keep this in mind as you read about what we did. If you find that you disagree with our methods or results, that's fine. It confirms the importance of using a method and format that you and your management will accept.

The Path to Proof

In our efforts, we learned four key things:

1. There is real proof.
2. Develop and follow a plan.
3. Adapt a methodology.
4. Report! Report! Report!

There Is Real Proof

For the nearly thirty combined years that the two authors have been involved in training, we know that training pays off. Never doubt that. The dollar return is there, and it is high.

Table 18.1. Incremental Sales Accounted for by Training (Specified Programs)

Mathematical Function		1	2 −	3 =	4 ÷	5 ×	6 =
Program	Month	Increased Sales Generated by Trained Regions	Increased Sales Generated by Untrained Regions	Incremental Sales Accounted for by Training	Number of Trained Regions	Total Number of Regions	Potential Incremental Sales with All Regions Trained
A1	August	$232,368	122,393	$109,975	10	28	$307,930
	September	$200,645	(198,062)	$398,707	11	28	$1,014,890
	October	($233,631)[a]	(16,820)	($206,812)[a]	15	28	($386,048)[a]
B1	October	$226,895	(280,435)	$507,330	12	28	$1,183,770
C1	November	$551,608	16,003	$535,605	13	28	$1,153,610
Total	5	$987,885	(356,920)	$1,344,805	NA	NA	$3,274,152

[a]Loss was due to extreme variation in several large regions that influenced the results negatively.

Table 18.2. Cumulative Data Year to Date

	Total	÷ Number	=	Average per Program per Month	×	Number of Effective Programs Released	=	Total Incremental Sales	× .20	=	Profit Contribution	÷	Cost of Training	=	ROI
Actual (Column 3)	$1,344,805	÷ 5	=	$268,962	×	11	=	$2,958,578	× .20	=	591,716	÷	95832	=	161%
Potential (Column 6)	$3,274,152	÷ 5	=	$654,830	×	11	=	$7,203,133	× .20	=	1,440,626	÷	95832	=	665%

Develop and Follow a Plan

Our efforts never really took off until we had a plan with objectives and actions. Our plan was simple but provided the direction that we needed to find an ROI of more than 85 percent for the year.

Adapt a Methodology

It's not hard. You do not need to be a statistician or to have an M.B.A. We used a lot of trial and error that you won't have to repeat. The pages that follow detail a simple method. Review them, and adapt the method to your organization.

Report! Report! Report!

Trainers know that training pays, but they have to share what they learn with everyone, especially field management. After the first report to Hobart Corporation, field management selected our department as one of four headquarters departments that best supported field sales. We gained their respect. We then made small fliers like the one shown in Figure 18.1. These fliers were included

Figure 18.1. Sample Training Pays Flier

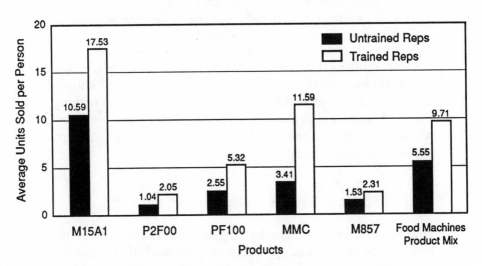

Note: Reps trained in food machines curriculum product training sold an average 4.15 units more per person than untrained reps.

in workbooks and other training materials to show participants the potential effect of training. These fliers had a huge impact on our sales representatives. Completion of training and test scores went way up. Reporting on all levels of evaluation works.

The Hobart Plan

Here are the details of exactly what and how we proved at Hobart that training pays.

In developing our plan, we agreed on one objective and three actions:

1. Objective: Increase the department's strategic (business) credibility by evaluating and reporting on the ROI of training.
2. Actions:
   a. Implement Kirkpatrick level 1, 2, and 3 evaluations in all programs.
   b. Report monthly on implementation of training by program and type of program, show number of additional programs, compare increase in test scores with figures from the previous year.
   c. Conduct a cost-benefit analysis of programs to determine level 4 results in ROI.

Developing evaluations of training was fairly simple. Many of our training programs already had reaction (level 1) and knowledge (level 2) measures. Completing the process was something that staff were able to accomplish quickly. However, we knew we needed to format and present our results as a business report, not an academic report.

Business Managers Report on Productivity

Find reports to use as examples. Try to attend business meetings where sales and marketing results are presented. If we couldn't get a member of our department to attend, one of us would go in after and collect the extra reports that are always left behind. In training lingo, we were finding SMEs and conducting a training analysis of our target population (senior management) to determine how to teach them that training pays.

Knowing how to relate to our target population and helped by examples of business reports, we talked with other managers (the SMEs) to learn method. The method that we used is not original. Since completing our bottom-line evaluation, we have contacted more than two hundred companies and found that they use basically the same types of data and method to determine business program results:

1. Volume and profits before the program, over several months or a year
2. Volume and profits over a three- to six-month time span after the program
3. The same data for a group not in the program
4. Detail in actual numbers and percentages on the difference.

It's best to select at least two groups from different parts of the country who received the training and two groups that did not. This will give your report the diversity that it needs to account for differences between regional markets and people.

Some math here will help to make it simple. Numbers and math are the language of business.

A = average prior sales for product X before sales reps received training. Label the time period *Time 1* and the trained rep group *T*.

B = average prior sales for product X for the T sales reps after receiving training. Label this *Time 2*.

C = average sales for a control group prior to training—same product, same time frame. This control group we'll call group C.

D = average sales (profits) for group C after the training. Use the same product and time frame for both groups.

E = Time 2 minus Time 1 in months

The formula itself is very simple:

$F = \frac{B-A}{E}$ = average additional sales (profit) for trained reps, per month, group E

$G = \frac{D-C}{E}$ = average additional sales (profit) for trained reps, per month, group C

$H = F - G$ = incremental sales (or profit) due to training

$I =$ estimated life of training benefit

$J = H \cdot I \cdot J$ = bottom-line contribution from training (total volume)

If you want to determine profit contribution from the bottom-line sales increase, multiply J by your company's profit margin. Changing the letters into numbers makes it come alive.

> Period of no training: January 1992–January 1993
> Training: January 1993
> Date of measure: June 1993
> A = 10,000   E = 5 months
> B = 30,000   I = 20 months
> C = 10,000
> D = 20,000
>
> $F = \frac{30,000 - 10,000}{5} = 4,000$
>
> $G = \frac{20,000 - 10,000}{5} = 2,000$
>
> H = 4,000 – 2,000 = 2,000
> K = 2,000 · 20 · 20 = 800,000

The profit margin for this product is 20 percent. $800,000 in increased dollar volume multiplied by 0.2 equals a bottom-line contribution from sales training of $160,000.

In my office is a sign that reads, *If you think training is expensive, try ignorance.* Every organization should be as concerned about the cost of training as it is about the cost of every other business program. The goal to achieve is for training to be considered just that: a business investment that the company cannot afford not to make. Finding and reporting on the payback of training demonstrates that it is like any other business investment and that, no doubt, training pays!

Chapter 19

Subjective Return on Investment

This case study from Hughes Aircraft Company describes an attempt to measure level 4 (results) in terms of ROI. Questionnaires were administered before and after training to the supervisors of participants in the training program. The study attempted to answer the question, Is whatever we are teaching doing us any good financially? The author identifies three reasons why a control group would not have been useful or even desirable. Although there is much subjectivity in the measurement approach, it shows how some types of training can be related to ROI.

Hughes Aircraft Company

Nicholas S. Merlo, Training Section Head, Ground Systems Group
Hughes Aircraft Company, Claremont, California

The concept of "return on investment" (ROI) is old hat in the business world. But until recently, its use in evaluating the effectiveness of management-training programs had been rare.

More and more, management is asking for evaluation that measures not only the practical utility of a program, but its financial utility and proven benefits as well. A growing need to justify the extensive management-training budget of Hughes Aircraft Company prompted its technical trainers to find a way to measure the overall effectiveness of training.

The following case study describes our evaluation and assessment of two existing training programs at Hughes. We asked supervisors to rate their employees' performance in each. We then used the results, which were quite impressive, to evaluate improvement and to estimate ROI. Estimating ROI posed a new challenge for our company, as it has for so many others. Described here are the procedures and rationale for data collection, along with three methods of calculating ROI.

How to Measure On-the-Job Performance

Training professionals differ on the difficulty of developing job-performance measures. Some say it's easy to develop objectives for skills training, but harder to objectify and measure learning in management-development programs. Having to justify costs and benefits of management-training programs can make forming realistic and quantifiable measures of on-the-job performance tough, they say.

The general literature, unfortunately, largely disagrees with this view and offers many simplistic, sometimes trivial, examples of how "easy" it is to measure job performance. Becker, for one, in an article in the book *Designing and Delivering Cost-Effective Training—and Measuring Results* (1977), says that such things as leading, problem-solving, deciding, analyzing, coaching, and goal-setting are "learnable, measurable managerial skills." Still, certain categories of managerial job performance are difficult to measure specifically, objectively, and quantifiably.

Therefore, some approaches for estimating ROI are based on subjective data, such as supervisors' opinions of employee performance. While less than ideal, subjective data can provide credible estimates of ROI. In these situations, one must describe clearly all assumptions and procedures that apply to the data collection, analysis and interpretation. Given such information, the people reviewing and evaluating the results may decide how credible the findings are, using their own criteria to determine the practical and financial utility of the particular training program.

Assessing Employee Performance

Participants

For this study, we selected twenty participants from non-management personnel in business-management job classifications. All were already enrolled in one of two Hughes Aircraft training classes. The target audience for these classes is employees in entry-level positions with approximately one year of experience. Theoretically, less experienced employees would be expected to derive the greatest benefit from such training classes; conversely, those with more than one year of experience would be expected to derive proportionately less benefit, by virtue of their job experience. It is important to note that most of the selected participants in this study had slightly more work experience, averaging 21 to 23 months on the job.

Training Classes

The first training class from which we selected participants was called "Earned Value." It compares actual costs of work (costs employers incur, expressed in dollars) with the amount of work performed, and the actual amount of performed work with the amount of planned work. The second class, called "Scheduling," helps trainees learn to develop work plans, define pieces of work, and set up time frames for accomplishing tasks. Eight participants were enrolled in Earned Value and 12 in Scheduling.

Questionnaires

To collect the performance data, we used pre-training and post-training questionnaires and asked supervisors to respond on the following issues concerning their employees' job performance:

- Overall performance (on a scale of one to five) on earned value or scheduling tasks

- Percent of time spent performing tasks
- Percent of errors or time spent reworking tasks
- Percent of time supervisor spent assisting employee on tasks
- Percent of time co-worker spent assisting with tasks
- Helpfulness or need of employee training in these two areas (on a scale of one to five)

Data Collection

We mailed pre-training questionnaires to the supervisor of each participant, to be completed and returned prior to the start of each class. Supervisors were not told they would receive a post-training questionnaire. We used the data from the completed pre-training questionnaires and the supervisors' ratings to establish a pre-training level of performance for each employee.

Six weeks after the completion of each class, we sent the post-training questionnaire to the supervisors. To assess the effects of the training programs on the supervisors' ratings of their employees' job performance, we compared the data from both sets of questionnaires. The results served as indicators of the practical utility of the training programs from the supervisors' perceptions of trainees' on-the-job performance of earned value or scheduling tasks. The bottom-line objective of this effort, however, was to assess the financial utility and ROI of the training.

Estimating Financial Utility

Method 1

We used three methods to estimate financial utility. The first method, described by Godkewitsch in a recent *Training* magazine article (May 1987), uses the following formula to compute the estimates:

$$F = N \ [(E \times M) - C]$$

where F = financial utility, N = number of people trained, E = effect of the training, M = monetary value of the effect, C = cost per person of the training.

The value of *E* used in this method represents the magnitude of the effect, expressed in standard deviations. It is derived by first computing the difference between the average of the pre- and post-training scores, and then dividing that difference by the standard deviation of the pre-training scores.

In this model, one standard deviation in performance is equivalent to 40 percent of the annual salary of those affected; therefore, *M* equals 40 percent of the average salary of target audience employees.

The per-person cost of training in this study (*C*) is based in three factors: instructor time, student time, and costs of training materials. The cost of developing the training program itself is not included in this analysis, as we included it in the ROI calculations. Further, the cost of facilities is not included, as these training programs were held in Hughes facilities and therefore did not incur costs often associated with training programs, such as hotel or conference facilities.

Method 2

The second method of estimating financial utility is a modification of the first. The formula used to obtain these estimates is

$$F = N \ [(t \times M!) - C \div B]$$

where *F* = financial utility, *N* = number of people trained, *t* = the value of statistic *t*, *M!* = *adjusted* monetary value of the training, *C* = cost per person of the training, *B* = benefit due to reduced supervisor and co-worker time.

To adjust for the relatively small sample sizes used in this study, we substituted the value of the statistic *t* for the variable *E*, which was used in Method 1. We derived the statistic *t* by applying the t-test to the data sets for overall performance on earned value tasks and on percentage of errors or tasks reworked. To adjust for the percent of time employees spent performing earned value or scheduling tasks, we substituted *M!* for *M* (that is, Godkewitsch's *M*, which represents 100 percent of an employee's time). In this study, however, we found that employees spent an average of 35 to 36 percent of their time on either scheduling or earned value tasks. Thus, *M!* represents 35 to 36 percent of the value of *M*.

Supervisors in this study estimated in advance that, after training, both they and the trainees' co-workers would spend less time helping the trainees with their earned value and scheduling tasks. Because these data could be converted readily into additional dollar savings, we accounted for this savings (*B*) in the financial utility estimates. We used the actual average annual salaries of supervisors and co-workers to compute *B*, based on the difference in the percentage of time supervisors estimated on the pre- and post-training questionnaires that they would spend on tasks.

Method 3

The final method used to estimate financial utility is based on factors that also lend "logical" support for estimating ROI. We used this formula:

$$F = N \; [(I \times M!!) - C + B]$$

where F = financial utility, N = number of people trained, I = performance rating improvement index, $M!!$ = adjusted monetary value of the training, C = cost per person of the training, B = benefit due to reduced supervisor and co-worker time.

In this method, the performance rating improvement index (*I*) represents the improvement (expressed as a percentage) in the supervisors' performance ratings of the employees. The adjusted monetary value of the effect (*M!!*) represents average annual salary as a function of time spent performing earned value or scheduling tasks—that is, 35 to 36 percent of the average annual salary of target audience employees.

From each method of computing financial utility, we generated two estimates for each training program: one using the overall performance on tasks data, and one using the percentage of errors/reworked data. We generated only one ROI estimate for each training program and used the more conservative financial utility estimate for each in our final evaluation.

Financial Utility Results

Table 19.1 shows the results of the financial utility analyses. The dollar values (expressed in millions of dollars) represent the esti-

Table 19.1. Estimates of Financial Utility

Method of Estimating	Earned Value Training		Scheduling Training	
	Overall Task Performance	*Percent Errors/Rework*	*Overall Task Performance*	*Percent Errors/Rework*
Method 1	$5.7M	$6.6M	$14.2M	$3.2M
Method 2	$12.0M	$11.8M	$12.8M	$9.8M
Method 3	$5.4M	$5.1M	$5.0M	$4.1M

Note: The figures are derived using each of the three methods described. Estimates in shaded areas were used to compute ROI estimates.

mated financial benefit to be derived annually, based on an average of 300 trainees per year, companywide. As shown in the figure, the estimates range from $3.2 million to $14.2 million, depending on how they are computed. Once again, these estimates do not include the initial costs of developing the courses, as the ROI estimates account for them. In addition, the costs of ongoing course maintenance (such as updates or corrections) are not included for reasons explained later.

Return on Investment

Calculating ROI is a relatively standard procedure in the business world: ROI equals benefits (expressed in dollars) minus costs. Divide the difference by the costs; then multiply the resulting value by 100 to express the value as a percent.

In this study, we took the values in the benefits portion of the equation from the financial utility estimates. We used the more conservative of the two estimates obtained for each training program (namely, $5.1 million and $3.2 million) to compute the ROI. Note that these estimates account for all significant cost factors (C) in the ROI equation, with the exception of the course development costs.

In this study, the estimated ROI obtained for the earned value and scheduling training programs were an impressive 3,050 percent and 3,227 percent performance improvement, respectively.

Assessing the Outcome

The results of an effort of this nature can surprise the uninitiated training professional. While the ROI estimates might at first seem optimistic, the approach used to obtain them was conservative and pragmatic. Perhaps a key lesson here is that an ROI analysis requires many of us to reorient our thinking. That is, while ROI ultimately is concerned with behavioral changes and the financial consequences of those changes, it is not tied to the issues inherent in internal or external validity, with which most of us are used to dealing.

ROI is relatively unconcerned with what is being taught. Instead, it requires us to shift our attention from "are we teaching the right things?" to "is whatever we're teaching doing us any good financially?" Sometimes the results of such questioning can be surprising, as they were in this study.

These results suggest that the benefits of training programs can be substantial. We should note, however, that our results stemmed from data based on performance ratings of employees who were somewhat more experienced than the target audience. At the same time, though, we used the lower salaries of the target audience to estimate the financial benefits of the programs. It follows that if similar data were obtained for employees with substantially less experience (and therefore proportionately less prior on-the-job knowledge), or if the higher salaries of the actual (more experienced) participants were used, then the estimated benefit, both practical and financial, could be even greater. Nevertheless, supervisors indicated that this training was highly beneficial to even these more experienced employees, as evidenced by the high ratings of the training programs (that is, 4.1 and 4.2, on a scale of one to five).

How Credible Are the Results?

In considering the possibility of an ROI of 3,050 percent or 3,227 percent, one reasonably might ask whether the figures are at all realistic or achievable. The key to judging the credibility of the results is to look at the data from which they derived and to ask, how valid are the supervisor's ratings? This is a legitimate concern, although a precise measure may never be known for certain. If, for the moment, we can take these data to be reliable and sufficient, we are still left to consider the credibility of the estimates based on their sheer magnitude.

In the literature, we found other examples of ROI studies with comparable, equally significant findings for performance studies on management training programs. In one instance, Paquet et al. in a May 1987 *Training & Development* article reported on the impact of a series of training courses for new supervisors at CIGNA Corporation. The assessments were expressed in terms of ROI (when the gains could be converted to dollars) and in terms of productivity (expressed as percentages when dollar figures could not be determined directly). Fourteen case studies yielded ROI estimates ranging from 730 to 4,500 percent, and productivity increases ranging from 5 to 80 percent. Thus, the estimates in the study at hand fall within the range of estimates reported by other authors for similar training programs. Even if these ROI estimates were in error by a factor of 100, Hughes still would have realized significant financial benefit from the training programs.

There are two other matters of concern regarding the credibility of ROI estimates: how are the course development costs in these ROI estimates included? and why are the ongoing course maintenance costs from the estimates omitted? With respect to the former, the value of the ROI obtained from the data and methodology in this study is based on the lowest, most conservative estimate possible of financial benefit obtained. We decided to account for the total cost of the initial course development in a single estimate, as opposed to amortizing this cost over a hypothetical period of time.

We omitted ongoing course maintenance costs for two reasons. First, these costs will vary from year to year, depending on various factors that can't be determined in advance, such as changes in the work environment, changes in the subject matter itself, or errors discovered and reported by students, instructors, or subject-matter experts. Second, if costs for course updates occur during a given year, they certainly will be less than the original course development cost. Recalculating the ROI estimate for such a year probably would yield a value that far exceeds the initial estimate.

Many studies of this nature use a "control group" to obtain comparative data for evaluating training effectiveness. I offer three comments on this practice.

First, all things being equal, an experimental design using a control group may indeed be superior to one without it, but pragmatic considerations often preclude such an approach. One problem involves the methods used to establish experimental and control groups. One method is to match subjects on the basis of whatever criteria seem appropriate, and then to assign one member of each matched pair to either the experimental or the control group. Another method is randomly to assign subjects to treatment conditions. Both methods are legitimate, but neither is practical for evaluating day-to-day business activities. Plus, most supervisors and employees aren't likely to be amenable to such arrangements.

Second, control-group evaluations might be reasonable in classroom situations where performance measures are based on uniform, validated test items. But in the real work environment, equivalent tasks (such as scheduling) routinely vary in nature and complexity, and are often difficult to quantify. Even where conditions and standards of task performance are equally variable, imposing the kind of structure required of even a rudimentary experimental design would so radically influence the purpose of the study (measuring actual task performance under actual job circumstances), that it would undermine the meaningfulness of the study and could result in generalized information.

Third, even though a control group might, under certain circumstances, provide a sounder basis for assessing the effect of a controlled variable such as training, the primary purpose of this study was to estimate the financial utility (specifically ROI) of the training programs. Within this context, the data that would be obtained from a control group would be of limited value, as these data don't help us calculate either the financial utility or the ROI estimates. In using the methods at hand, we presume that the effect of a training intervention does, in fact, account for the differences observed between pre- and post-training performance to the extent necessary for making prudent use of the estimates thus derived.

This type of study is not a true experiment. While using a control group might establish a "better" measure of the "true" magnitude of the effect of a training program, our process—the use of a one-group, pre-test/post-test design, with known limitations, and the use of the appropriate statistic for analysis and the subsequent interpretation—is adequate. The issue, then, may be reduced to what constitutes an adequate or pragmatic design, versus what might constitute a "better" design. In this case, the methods used are sufficient and significant.

Chapter 20

The Bottom Line

The evaluators in this case study developed a concept called the *impact model*. The model has four elements: opinions (reaction), learning, behavior, and results. The evaluation sought to answer the question, Does management training result in improved productivity in the manager's workplace? Therefore, although the evaluation included level 3, it concentrated on level 4—the authors called it the *bottom line*. They proceeded on the assumption that the intended outcome of management training is improved productivity in the workplace. The training program emphasized this fact, and the evaluation tried to find out whether it really happened. The study compares the costs of the program with its results to establish return on investment.

CIGNA Corporation

Basil Paquet, Assistant Director
Corporate Management Development and Training
CIGNA Corporation, Hartford, Connecticut

Reprinted from *Training & Development*. Copyright by the American Society for Training and Development. Reprinted with permission. All rights reserved.

Elizabeth Kasl, Adjunct Professor of Adult Education
Teachers College, Columbia University, New York, New York

Laurence Weinstein, Associate Professor of Management
Sacred Heart University, Bridgeport, Connecticut

William Waite, Vice President
Corporate Management Development and Training
CIGNA Corporation, Hartford, Connecticut

Most HRD practitioners believe that management training makes a real difference in the workplace, but many of us avoid proving it. However at CIGNA Corporation's corporate management development and training (CMD&T), which provides training for employees of CIGNA Corporation's operating subsidiaries, we set out to do just that — prove that our management training makes a real business contribution. We wagered that an investment of creativity, hard work, and some budget dollars would pay handsome dividends for our organization.

For the sake of brevity, we will describe just three of the 14 in-depth cases from our pilot study showing how managers used their training to improve productivity. These three cases reflect savings and income totaling $280,000, or two-thirds of the full cost of training the entire population who were involved in that program for the full year — including participants' salaries, overhead, and program development costs.

Since our companies operate in a profit-oriented environment where results are the measure of ultimate worth, our CMD&T evaluation team reasoned that if we were going to provide our training's worth, then we should use management's own language — business results and return-on-investment. That meant we needed to show that management training could be linked directly to improved productivity in the workplace. If we could create a bottom-line impact evaluation, we believed we would benefit in our efforts to

- Justify the worth and budget of the training group to top management
- Market our training products and services to our internal clients
- Redesign our programs and develop new ones

Targeting Productivity Results

Perhaps the primary reason proving the bottom-line impact of management training is not easy is that, like the managers you train, you achieve results through others—in this case, your trainees. We began by setting up some guidelines for our work. First we took a hard look at what an impact evaluation is supposed to accomplish. Generally speaking impact evaluation is the study of whether an educational intervention brings about intended results. Reformulated to fit our business environment, the question became, "Does management training result in improved productivity in the manager's workplace?"

The question was straightforward and suggested our first guideline: Our evaluation would have to follow the manager back to the workplace in order to find out if the work unit's productivity improved after the manager attended training.

Second we took a hard look at what it means to conduct evaluation research in a profit-oriented business environment. We realized that we couldn't expect people to put much time into helping with the research unless they were also benefitting in some way. We also recognized that any viable strategy for ongoing impact evaluation needed to be cost-effective for CMD&T budget and staff time.

These two considerations led us to establish our second guideline: Impact evaluation data collection needed to be built into the training program itself. This strategy addressed both of our concerns. If managers could use the evaluation data for their own benefit as part of their training, they would be more likely to cooperate. If data were collected as part of an on-going training assignment, CMD&T staff would be spared the time-consuming effort of adding a new activity—evaluation data collection—to already busy schedules.

As our impact project was getting under way, it fortuitously happened that another CMD&T project team was redesigning the training program that CIGNA offers to all new first-level to mid-level subsidiary managers, Basic Management Skills (BMS). Our two teams joined forces, working together to embed the framework for impact evaluation into the new program design.

The BMS program was an ideal choice for the impact evaluation project. Its curriculum included a broad range of management skills that, if practiced in the workplace, should have an impact on work-unit productivity. Content areas included planning, problem solving, motivating direct reports, communication, leadership, delegation, performance appraisal, plus a host of corporate human resource management policies and procedures ranging from compensation administration through employment practices.

CMD&T already had positive feedback on this program. Since its inception, BMS had received superior ratings on the "smile sheets" collected from the trainees. Every staffperson who had provided training during the program had been stopped in a hallway or the company dining room by happy graduates with success stories to share. All we needed to do was transform intuitive beliefs and anecdotal evidence into bottom-line language.

The Chain of Impact

The linkage between training and workplace results takes place through a chain reaction along the levels of impact. Training changes the participant's attitudes and knowledge so that the participant is then able to change his or her management behavior back on the job. If the training has targeted appropriate behaviors, then a change in those behaviors produces the results intended — improved work-unit productivity in the case of a management program like BMS.

Each link in the chain of impact can provide evaluative feedback about the training program. The further along the chain the information is, the more removed it gets from the training experience and the more difficult it is to obtain. But along with that difficulty comes the power to show bottom-line results. Each step on the chain of impact moves us closer to proof that the training is making a real impact on the corporation.

The decision of when and how to measure these types of change is the task of any impact evaluation design team. Table 20.1 summarizes the design our team produced.

The first level of information — participant opinions about the job-relatedness and effectiveness of the training — we obtain by

Table 20.1. CIGNA CMD&T Impact Model

Chain of Impact		Research Tool		Time Period
Opinions	▼ D i f f i c u l t y ▼	Trainee self-report	P o w e r	Throughout training and at three-month follow-up
Learning		Trainee self-report		At end of training
Behavior		Survey of trainee's subordinates		Before training and at three-month follow-up
Results		Trainee's work unit records, action plan, and BMS workbook		Tracked from three months preceding training to three months following training

asking trainees to rate the content areas. We do this throughout the BMS program.

The next level is knowledge, skill, or attitude acquisition. Trainees complete an overall program evaluation that collects information on what they have learned.

The next link in the chain of impact is behavior back in the workplace. Our evaluation uses a survey of the trainee's direct reports. This scale measures employee observations of manager behavior in the BMS content areas of planning, leadership, motivation, performance management discussions, setting clear performance standards, and the work unit's communications environment. We survey the direct reports before management training begins and three months after the training has been completed and the manager is back on the job.

Finally the last critical step: We base our results on repeated measures of work-unit performance *before* and *after* training. We directly relate these measures to productivity action plans created during the management training and base them on actual business records.

Let us be clear that CMD&T did not set out to prove scientifically that the chain of impact exists. And though we did observe strict research methods, CMD&T is not a research unit and

CIGNA is not a laboratory. We laid out a model on the types and possible timing of evaluation data and collection to clarify for ourselves what might be possible to accomplish. The business results that trainees achieved exceeded our expectations. Without a model and methodology we never could have documented these results.

Designing Evaluation In

In its original form, the program included twelve training days. The project team working on the new training design had been charged with lowering costs by reducing the program to six days: one overview session and a five-day training week. To facilitate this reduction in time without shortchanging the skills training that had made this program so successful, all the corporate policy material was moved into a self-study workbook for trainees to complete before attending the group sessions.

Building our impact evaluation model into BMS required major design changes in addition to those already planned. We radically redesigned the planning and productivity modules, added a follow-up day, created a pre-posttraining survey of management behavior, and made other changes that made an outstanding program stronger still.

Results: Changes in Behavior

Our BMS training makes a difference in management behaviors. Our pre-posttest data from the new management skills survey backs us up.

The survey consists of thirty-six Likert-type five-point scale items that are used to create seven different indices. Six of these indices measure the manager's behavior, and the seventh measures general organizational climate for which the manager is not necessarily responsible. The six behavior indices are related to separate content units in the BMS training design and are reported to the trainee as separate scores in order to help that trainee set personal learning objectives.

Because the intercorrelation among the six scales is relatively high, for the purpose of impact evaluation they are treated as one global measure. The six indices are weighted equally and combined into one grand mean, referred to in this report as "Manager Behavior." The seventh scale is called "General Climate." The average intercorrelation among the six scales is $r = .75$. The correlation between Manager Behavior and General Climate is $r = .57$. Statistical properties are based on $N = 427$. Trainees in the management program the year before the new design was launched were used for the developmental work.

Our impact evaluation uses these scales for three different comparisons. Time 1 is before training and Time 2 is after training. Comparison 1 equals Time 1 minus Time 2 on Manager Behavior, Comparison 2 equals Time 1 minus Time 2 on General Climate, and Comparison 3 equals Comparison 1 minus Comparison 2.

The five-point scales assign *1* to the most positive opinion and *5* to the most negative. A positive difference for Comparisons 1 and 2 indicates a positive change, respectively, in Manager Behavior and General Climate. Comparison 3 is important because we need to know that if there is a change in General Climate, this change alone is not the sole cause of a change in productivity. Thus it is important for Comparison 3 to be positive and significant.

We are not arguing here that climate is immaterial to performance. To the contrary we trust that long-term positive changes in behavior will affect climate, which ought to in turn affect performance. Our immediate objective is, however, to change behavior, and it is those shifts we measure in our pre-posttesting by using Comparison 3 to factor out general climatic factors that might obscure behavior change.

Table 20.2 demonstrates that when the first three sessions of BMS were analyzed as a group, the three comparisons support the assertion that training makes a positive difference in the manager's behavior. Further the data indicates that if these managers' work units improve their productivity, that improvement is likely to be linked to the manager's behavior and not to other climate factors in the corporation.

Table 20.2. Comparisons of Manager Behavior and
General Climate for First Three Sessions of Basic Management Skills

	Comparison #1	Comparison #2	Comparison #3
	Manager Behavior Time 1–Time 2	General Climate Time 1–Time 2	Manager Change– Climate Change
N[a]	22	22	22
Ex	3.40	−0.51	3.91
Ex²	3.3512	6.9503	3.0565
x	0.155	−0.023	0.178
	$t = 1.98$	$t = 0.19$	$t = 2.49$
	$p < .05$	$p = $ n.s.	$p < .025$

[a]BMS participants are included in this analysis only when the Time 1–Time 2 comparison of matched surveys is based on two or more employee opinions. Five participants who have only one employee matched at Time 1 and Time 2 are deleted from this comparison.

Individualizing Productivity Measures

When challenged to measure results in management's productivity-oriented language, we took a bold and startlingly simple step: we decided to measure productivity in the work unit.

As noted in the start-up phase of the project, the productivity that counts is what takes place in the trainee's individual work unit. Since it could never be cost effective to send a team of data-gathering evaluators to each graduate's work unit, we set out to design into BMS the mechanism by which each trainee would provide us with the needed data.

We call our strategy "individualizing productivity measures" and we believe that it achieves a type of validity in impact evaluation that most strategies fail to reach. As set forth in our start-up phase, our efforts are predicated on the assumption that the intended outcome of management training is improved productivity in the workplace. From this assumption it follows that the most valid measure of management training's impact is a measure of workplace productivity.

Our impact evaluation methodology demands that a management program set out to affect productivity in both method and purpose. Linkage to training occurs in the specific case of our BMS program, for example, because

- Productivity is a central focus of this management training program.
- Participants are taught how to create productivity measures as part of their training.
- Participants are also taught how to use productivity data as performance feedback and as support for performance goal setting.
- Participants write a productivity action plan as part of their training, and are contracted to bring back measurable results to a follow-up session.
- Individualized productivity measures (IPMs) are put in place as part of the action plan. IPMs are tailored to measure plan results specifically, accurately, and objectively.

These steps ensure core validity; the strongest proof of the true impact of training will be found by measuring the productivity of the trainee's work unit. In a large corporation, where trainees in a management skills course come from a variety of production and staff environments, a measure of impact that has core validity by definition *must vary from manager to manager.*

Thus we have gone in the opposite direction of most HRD practitioners who have sought to prove the results of training. We believe that those who track absenteeism, turnover, morale, and promotion patterns limit their measures to surrogate results. True bottom-line results are found in the work records of the individual participants and their units.

Training People to Demonstrate Results

As part of their training, BMS participants are required to follow step-by-step workbook procedures that lead them through a thorough analysis of their unit from both a technical or work management perspective and from a human resource management perspective. It also initiates a systematic approach to planned changes that will positively affect their units' business results.

Previously we believed it was enough to teach good planning and problem solving, with evaluation embedded in the planning model. We discovered, however, that the majority of new managers did not know the rudimentary techniques of work measurement and writing performance standards for both their units and individual workers. Management by objectives, performance management, and productivity were abstractions for our first-level management population. We discovered—and it was a revelation despite how obvious it seems—that we could not prove results if our trainees did not know how to document them, and that they were far less likely to produce them if they did not know how to use productivity measurement as a management tool.

So we devised training materials that teach managers how to write performance standards for both their units and individual performers; how to use simplified work measurement techniques; how essential performance management is used as a tool to complement management by objectives, positive reinforcement, and constructive feedback on performance; and other essentials of good management. Measuring the results of their action plans becomes as important to our trainees as obtaining these data is to us, the training department.

The principle is simple. Many managers never go beyond measuring performance in terms of production. We push our trainees to establish standards and to create true measures of productivity based on this familiar formula: Divide your output by a partial factor of input consumed to produce that product or service.

These measures and the action plans they will track are reviewed and critiqued by fellow trainees and trainers during the BMS action planning module, which lasts a full day. Participants are challenged to produce the best plans and measures possible. Then they are required to go back to their work records and establish a base period of performance for at least three months prior to their training and action plan. When they leave training they implement their plans, track progress, and deliver their results sixteen weeks later at a follow-up session. Before, during, and after the training we will have cycled the trainees through our impact model at all levels.

Business Results

Table 20.3 is a set of case studies representing two BMS pilot groups whose results CMD&T studied. In some cases the business impact can be converted into dollars. In others it is reported as productivity gains. In all cases these managers were asked to produce verifiable results based on actual work-unit records to support pre-posttraining and measures of performance.

In a fast-paced business environment, a lot of changes can occur in a quarter of a year. Many CIGNA company trainees change their jobs and sometimes their jobs change. About two-thirds of our trainees return for the follow-up; about one-half the original class gets the opportunity to see their action plans through to completion. For many of our trainees their business reality changes so significantly within a quarter of a year that tracing their IPM results loses its validity.

We have compared all relevant demographics on managers who provide follow-up data with those who do not. We are unable to detect any differences and do not think self-selection is biasing our results.

Because our IPM methodology creates different results for each participant, it does not lend itself easily to summary analysis or inferential statistics. Right now our cases rest on their own merits as narratives of actual results. There is considerable power in realizing that a handful of trainees contribute enough savings and income from the success of their BMS action plans to fund the training of an entire managerial population for a full year.

But we do think that inferential analysis is possible. By randomly selecting a subset of trainees, results could be classified according to degree of success, links could be established between productivity data and behavior-change measures, and inferences could be drawn to the entire BMS population.

Such an inferential analysis might reveal powerful data, but it is also considerably more research-based than a functional management training unit like CMD&T can probably afford to pursue, and it is unlikely we will decide to fund such an extension of our study. For now, we will continue to collect case study results for the illustrations they draw of the business results that management training can generate. We also are eager to examine

Table 20.3. BMS Case Studies on Bottom-Line Results

Case No.	Manager Function	Plan Results
1	Reinsurance coding unit	18 K in savings, 730% ROI
2	Premium collections	80 K increased investment income, 3, 100% ROI
3	Premium collections	150 K increased investment income, 5,900% ROI
4	Exchange department	95 K increased revenue, 4,475% ROI
5	Benefits administration	60% improvement on timing standard
6	Benefits administration	80% improvement on accuracy standard
7	Benefits administration	80% improvement on accuracy standard
8	Systems processing unit	20% productivity increase, 110 K in budget savings, 4,500% ROI, plus increased tape mounts, improved turn-around on service requests
9	Financial analysis unit	35% improvement on on-time service, plus 25% productivity increase on job set-ups
10	Systems testing unit	165% efficiency increase against production standard
11	Actuarial unit	15% improvement on timing standard, 70% improvement in accuracy while production volume increased by 20%, no staff increases
12	Actuarial unit	15% improvement in on-time reporting, 30% increase in quality review standard
13	Actuarial unit	30% increase on service timing and 10% improvement in accuracy standard
14	Actuarial unit	5% increase on service timing and 10% improvement in accuracy standard

larger sets of data on behavior change as measured by our survey instrument.

Details from three of our case studies can illustrate how trainees use a synergistic application of BMS-learned skills along with their action plans and IPMs to create and document productivity changes.

Case One

In this case, the manager of a reinsurance coding unit confronted problems with processing backlogs, work-flow bottlenecks, work distribution issues, and morale. This manager tackled them head-on in her BMS productivity action plan. She created new standards, increased individual worker responsibility, and streamlined the work flow and processing sequence for her unit.

To measure her action plan results in true productivity terms, she divided a weighted production output—number of cases produced multiplied by a weight representing the degree of case difficulty—by the total available worker days in a given month, thus factoring out vacation time as well as time spent by staff on other kinds of unit production. Bottom-line results in six months showed that every productivity goal for each worker and the entire unit had been achieved or surpassed.

Figure 20.1 illustrates both productivity and production charts for a six-month period. Notice in this manager's case the difference between measuring productivity and production. Had she been monitoring only production, as was her practice before BMS training, she would not have understood that her unit was performing well in spite of the severe staffing problems in October.

Based on calculations using salary and fringe for the unit, net improvements equaled $18,000 in savings, for an ROI of 730 percent on the cost of training this manager. In most cases an ROI estimate based on the value of partial input instead of output is an underestimate of actual benefits to the company. Even with the underestimate this manager was pleased with the estimate of her action plan's bottom-line value. She noted that $18,000 was approximately the cost of hiring a new worker and realized, with satisfaction, that hiring a new worker had been her boss' original idea for solving the backlog problem.

Case Three

This case features a premium collections manager. Collecting premiums on time is important in our business because late premiums represent a lost investment opportunity. Through survey feedback from her subordinates this manager learned her problems were largely due to poor human resource management

Figure 20.1. Productivity and Production in the Reinsurance Unit

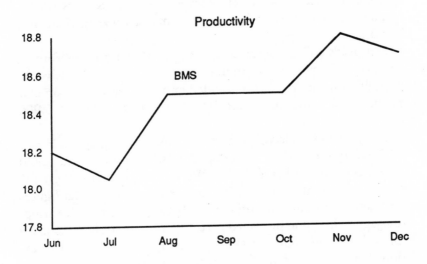

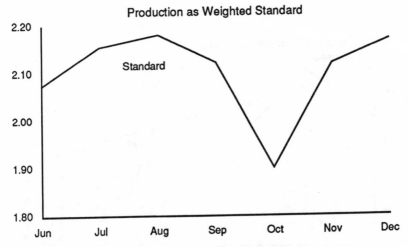

Note: Productivity = production ÷ total available worker days.
Weighted production = weight factor (degree of difficulty) × number processed
$18K savings; 730% ROI

skills and failure to set clear performance goals. In-depth post-training interviews with her workers by CMD&T revealed a manager who dramatically altered numerous management behaviors.

Her unit's collection rate also changed dramatically — from an average of 75 percent of premium on time to an impressive 96 percent. This improvement yielded extra investment income of $150,000 per annum, for an ROI on training dollars of 5,900 percent.

The premium collection manager's productivity graph in Figure 20.2 is very interesting. She asked us to project where she would have been *without* her training. We plotted a "line of best fit" projected from her unit's baseline performance. The dollar figures represent premium value differences between actual performance (the jagged line) and projected performance (the straight line). We think this is a good illustration of training's value versus the notion that a manager would "get there anyway."

Figure 20.2. Improvement in Premium Collections

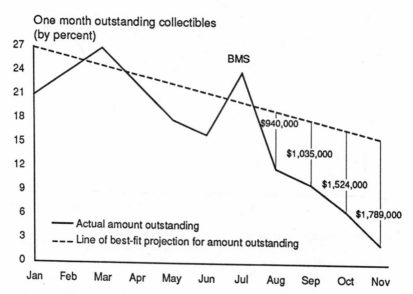

Note: Productivity = total number of premiums collected ÷ total number of premiums due
    $150K increased income; 5,900% ROI

Case Eight

In our final example, a systems manager who ran agency paycycle reports and processed a variety of service requests targeted the efficient use of analyst–programmer (A–P) time to reduce the down-time involved in respecifying, researching, and testing projects that had been improperly set up. He and his boss were looking for small improvements, but they agreed the action plan would be tackled aggressively. The results, as shown in Figure 20.3, were a 20 percent productivity increase that bottom-lined at $112,000 in savings on the budget, for a 4,500 percent ROI of training dollars.

Figure 20.3. Analyst-Programmer Utilization Index

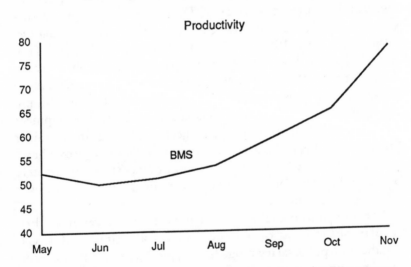

Note: Productivity = analyst-programmer hours used ÷ analyst-programmer hours available
$110 K savings; 4,500% ROI

The IPM used to track plan results was a calculation of A–P hours used divided by A–P hours available; this generated an A–P utilization-efficiency index. Productivity spin-offs included an increase in the average percent of tape mounts per month and a decrease in the average number of days it took to turn around client service requests. It's worth noting that management reinforcement of training was present in this case.

We have built into BMS numerous opportunities for joint discussion, planning, and actions by the trainee and his or her manager. Such reinforcement contact increases the likelihood of both changed behavior and actual plan results.

Calculating Return-on-Investment

When we were able to price the value of an action plan, we then could calculate ROI for the corporation.

The two halves of the ROI equation are benefits and costs; ROI equals benefits minus costs divided by costs. We used a model for calculating training costs that has been described by two of the authors in previous issues of *Training & Development* (Weinstein, L. M. "Collecting Training Cost Data," *Training and Development,* August 1982, pp. 30–34; Weinstein, L. M., and Kasl, E. S. "How the Training Dollar Is Spent," *Training and Development,* October 1982, pp. 90–96). This cost estimate is much more complete than those usually accounted for in a typical training department budget. We include classroom, program development (amortized, in this case, over a projected 25 programs), trainer preparation time, general administration, and corporate overhead.

Altogether one BMS seven-day program costs approximately $11,850. Figuring an average of 20 trainees per session, this is about $590 per person.

For some purposes the time spent by trainees away from their regular jobs is a cost of training, so we also estimated this. Using the mid-point salary range for a typical participant job grade, and figuring in 24.4 percent fringe, we compute a worth of $145 per day for each BMS participant. This generates a lost-time cost of $1,015 per participant and $20,300 per program.

When costs of $1,600 per participant are compared to some of the dollar values we were able to attach to action plans, the ROI leaves little doubt that the program produces amply.

Chapter 21

Making a Play for
Training Evaluation

This article appeared in the April 1994 issue of *Training and Development,* which is published by the American Society for Training and Development. It describes the four levels and how each can be applied. The company, Montac, is hypothetical and provides the setting for a practical discussion on evaluation between a training specialist and the head of the training department. The article, which is well written, describes the benefits and the importance of each level.

Montac, A Fictitious Company

Theodore Krein and Katherine Weldon
Instructional Design Department
Ernst & Young, Vienna, Virginia

The setting is the corporate headquarters of Montac, a hypothetical diversified company with many divisions. Mary Hoskins is Montac's training director. She is based at corporate headquarters, but her staff provides support to all divisions.

In addition to developing and administering some programs that are available to employees throughout the corporation, Mary's staff provides internal consulting on improving performance. Often the consulting leads to the development of training programs specific to the needs of a division. The consulting may also result in recommendations for nontraining solutions to performance problems.

Pete Elston is a training specialist on Mary's staff. He joined the company six months ago, after graduating with a liberal-arts degree from the local university. Mary hired Pete because she saw real potential in him. His education did not include courses in learning design, but Mary was convinced that she could develop Pete into a competent training professional—sort of a Pygmalion story. In addition to encouraging Pete to take courses in instructional technology at night, Mary has made it her personal mission to coach Pete.

Under Mary's guidance, Pete has been working on a performance-improvement project for the Granville Division of Montac. He has completed the front-end analysis and has prepared a set of potential performance objectives to be achieved by a training program, which has yet to be developed. We enter the scene as Pete enters Mary's office.

Pete Elston Reporting

Pete   Mary, you asked me to check back with you after the design meeting with the client, once we had the objectives pretty well developed. As you know, we determined that the problems at Granville are caused by a lack of knowledge and skill. So training seems to be an appropriate way to overcome the performance gap.

Mary   You've done a great job of expressing most of your objectives in performance terms. That will be important as we move ahead with this project. When we state objectives in performance language, it's easier to know for sure whether we've achieved them. The reason I wanted to meet with you today is to begin discussing the evaluation plan for your program.

Pete Isn't it premature to talk about evaluation so early? I haven't even begun developing the program.

Mary I know what you mean. We usually think of evaluation happening *after* we hold a training program, so it must seem as if we're jumping the gun by talking about evaluation now. But here's why we're not.

The jargon of our profession includes two general terms—summative evaluation and formative evaluation. In today's meeting we'll concentrate on summative evaluation. This is evaluation of a program after it's been offered, to learn whether the training achieved what we wanted it to achieve. But I also want you to be aware of formative evaluation.

Formative evaluation involves checks we make during the program-development process to make sure that the program will meet our criteria of excellence. One formative evaluation technique is to have another experienced training professional go over the initial draft of a training design. That reviewer can consider a lot of different criteria, including the design's appropriateness for achieving the program's objectives.

We can take several other steps during development that increase the likelihood that participants will learn what we want them to learn. For example, we might test a case study on some experienced staff to see if it makes sense to them. Is it relevant to their jobs? Is it consistent with the company's culture? Do the instructions make sense?

When we get into program development, we will talk about the kinds of formative evaluation that might be appropriate for our program. For now, let's get back to the topic at hand—evaluation after the fact.

Program Objectives Versus the Ultimate Objectives

Pete You said we needed to develop an evaluation plan. What did you have in mind?

Mary What outcomes do you want from your program?

Pete I want the program to achieve the objectives we have on my list. For example, here's one of them: "At the end of the program, the new market-research analyst will be able to conduct an interview to determine what the client wants to learn from the market study."

Mary   At what point do you want participants to show they can do these things? I mean, is this an objective you can check on at the end of the course, or does it apply to what these analysts will do when they return to their jobs?

Pete   I guess I want it to be both. I'd like to know at the end of the course that they have met the objectives and can perform the skills. If they can, I can assume they'll be able to do them on the job.

Mary   I know that seems logical. But there's a catch. It's true that your ultimate objective is to influence job performance. That's always our intent—usually assumed, but seldom stated—when we create a training program. At the moment the program is finished, we can't know whether it really will be successful in improving job performance. The best we can tell at the end of the program is whether the participants learned what they were supposed to learn.

We use our best judgment and experience to design training that will have an on-the-job impact. We want transfer of learning to the job. But at times, even our best judgment fails us, and we don't get the ultimate outcomes we want.

Pete   So you're telling me that I can't know whether my training really has an impact?

Four Levels of Evaluation

Mary   What I'm saying is you can't know at the end of the program whether it will have the desired on-the-job effects. Let me give you a scheme for evaluating programs. Donald Kirkpatrick developed it at the University of Wisconsin. He described four levels of evaluating training:

- Level 1—how participants reacted to the program
- Level 2—what participants learned from the program
- Level 3—whether what was learned is being applied on the job
- Level 4—whether that application is achieving results

Pete   I didn't know there could be so much to evaluation. To be honest, I didn't know there was so much involved in putting together training programs. It wasn't all that long ago that I assumed someone would just sit down and figure out all the topics a program should cover, develop a bunch of lectures to cover the topics, and then go ahead and put on the course. It was a new experience for me when you spent all that time showing me how to arrive at performance objectives. And we still haven't begun developing the program.

Mary   Billions of dollars are spent each year in the United States on training. Much of that money is wasted because many trainers don't know the appropriate steps to take to ensure that their training addresses a real business need. And they don't know how to check to see whether that business need has been satisfied. In between those two are many other steps that are required if we are to do a truly professional job in training.

Pete   You mentioned the four levels. I recently spoke with somebody who said that Level 1 evaluation really isn't worth much. Now that you've described the other levels, I can see why he might feel that way.

Mary   Each of the four levels has value. The mistake many people make about Level 1 is to assume that if they get favorable participant reactions to their program, then that's all they need to conclude it's effective. It's not that Level 1 evaluation does not have value. It's a matter of recognizing what the value is—and what the limitations are.

Level 1: Reacting to Training

Mary   First, let's see what Level 1 evaluation can do for us. We'll look at five possible advantages:

- Level 1 can tell us how relevant participants thought the training was.
- It can tell us whether they were confused by any of the training.
- It can point out any areas in which trainees thought information was missing.

- It can give us an idea of how engaged the trainees felt by the training.
- It can tell us how favorable overall participant reactions were.

By the way, Pete, I don't mean to imply that this is all we can get from Level 1 evaluation. But these five information items should make my point.

First, relevance. We know that adults learn better when they can relate a presentation to their previous experience and when they can see the relevance of the program to their jobs. Most adults are serious enough about their jobs that they do not welcome attending a program they perceive to be a waste of time. If the program will not help them to do their jobs better, then they probably won't be pleased with it. We shouldn't be pleased with it, either.

Second is potential participant confusion. Are participants having trouble understanding the concepts we're trying to teach them? If there are places in the program where that's a problem, then we need to know about it. If, in their evaluation comments, several participants report similar points of confusion, then we have gained valuable information to help us make corrections—either in the program design, or in its delivery.

Summative evaluations—those that come at the end of a program—can be used to make improvements in the program. But when we use summative evaluation to improve a program, the evaluation also is formative. Some people argue that all evaluation is formative evaluation, since it's hard to imagine not making changes to a program when we discover deficiencies in midstream.

The third benefit of Level 1 evaluation is its potential for pointing out missing content areas. Participants are usually painfully aware of problems they have when they try to perform their jobs. Many expect the training to provide solutions to those problems. It is useful for us to know whether the training has failed to provide those solutions.

Don't let me mislead you. I'm not necessarily talking about missing instructional content in a program. Problems in this area might simply mean that we failed to clearly communicate what participants should expect from the program. It might also tell us that there are participant needs that can be addressed in some other way.

Fourth, did participants feel engaged? We know that adults learn better when they are involved in the learning process than when they feel like passive targets of information dumping. If they did not feel involved in the training program, then their learning probably wasn't what we'd like it to be. We'd want to take a look at why. Is it a fault of the design, a fault of the presentation, or a combination of the two?

The fifth factor is how favorable participants felt toward the program as a whole. Often we can infer this from their answers to other questions. Merely learning that participants did not like the program isn't very helpful to us. It doesn't tell us what we might do about it. So we need participants to give us some specifics.

Participants' favorable feelings don't ensure learning. But they can influence the chances that there will be a market for the program in the future. Bad press can scuttle a program, even one that teaches valuable knowledge and skills.

So you see, it is useful to gather Level 1 evaluation information.

Level 2: Learning from Training

Pete   What happens in Level 2 evaluation?

Mary   This is where we check to see whether participants can perform according to the course objectives. And an important key to measuring the performance after training is stating the desired performance properly, during training.

Let's look at the objective you chose earlier: "The new market-research analyst will be able to conduct an interview to determine what the client wants to learn from the market study."

How might we be able to tell—during the training program—whether the new market-research analyst can conduct that interview?

Pete   It seems to me we could create a simulation role play—in which we ask the participant to conduct a simulated interview. We could watch the participant and judge whether she or he performed well.

Mary   Good. But I want to make sure there's no confusion here between on-the-job performance — ultimate performance — and performance at the end of the training program. So let's add some information on measurement to the description of that objective. We might restate the objective to incorporate measurement like this:

"Given a role play that simulates an interview with a client, the new market-research analyst will be able to conduct the interview to determine what the client wants to learn from the market study."

Now we have spelled out the conditions under which we can check to see whether the participant can satisfy the objective.

Pete   We might even create a checklist to use in evaluating the role-play performance.

Mary   That would be a great idea. We could include in that checklist all the specific interviewing principles we want the participant to demonstrate in the interview. Then we could add to our performance objective a criterion of satisfactory performance in the role play. Then the objective might look like this:

"Given a role play that simulates an interview with a client, the new market-research analyst will be able to conduct the interview to determine what the client wants to learn from the market study, demonstrating at least eight of the 10 interviewing principles presented in the training program."

Pete   As I recall, that would be a test to learn whether the participant could apply what he or she learned in class. And I guess the checklist would help guarantee that the same evaluation standard would be used to evaluate the interview performance of each program participant.

Mary   You're grasping this stuff very quickly, Pete. Now, you have some other objectives for your program that refer to the participant's knowledge of the subject. Let's look at a couple of them:

- "The participant will be able to explain the difference between a product-centered approach to selling and a client-centered approach to selling."

- "The participant will be able to recognize the five indicators of client resistance and the principal response to each."

Remember, we want to be able to tell, either during the training program or at the very end of the program, whether we have achieved these objectives. Look carefully at each and tell me what you would do to determine whether we have achieved them.

Pete   For the first one, we could ask the participant to explain to the program leader the difference between a product-centered approach and a client-centered approach.

Mary   Good. We see objectives like this for many classroom courses. Many program leaders never conduct that actual test. Instead, a leader judges the class's performance from his or her impressions of participants' understanding in class discussion.

That may be OK if the objective isn't crucial. But if we've spent the time analyzing what participants need in order to do their jobs, and we've included this objective in our program because it is important, then it's worth the effort to find out whether individual participants achieved the objective.

A key point to remember is that the verb we choose for a performance objective usually makes clear how we can test the performance. In this case, the verb is *explain*. So the participant must explain. It's clear that a true/false or multiple-choice question would not be adequate for measuring that performance. Instead, the participant would need to explain the differences between the two approaches—verbally, or in a short written paragraph.

Pete   The second objective we listed is about being able to recognize the five indicators of resistance and the responses to them. That one looks trickier, because it involves two different performances.

Mary   That's right. It is best to state each objective so that it contains only a single performance. So we probably should break this objective in two. But just for fun, let's see whether we could create a test item that would satisfy both parts of this objective. Start with the verb—*to recognize*. Now, what would—or wouldn't—we have participants do if we want them to recognize something?

Pete   Well, the objective suggests that they should know it when they see it. It doesn't require them to write a sentence or even to drag something out of their memories with any clues other than the key words in the objective.

So what would a test item look like that asks for recognition? The question would contain the items we want trainees to recognize. So if it's a paper-and-pencil test, the five indicators would appear on the printed page. I suppose we could present the five indicators and ask, "Are these the five indicators?" But that makes the question require only a simple yes-no response. And half the participants could get it right by guessing. That wouldn't give us much comfort that participants had learned what we want them to learn about the indicators.

What if we listed ten items, including the five indicators, and asked the participants to pick out the five? I think that would be a better question.

Mary   I agree. And if that were all we wanted to know, that question would do the job. But we also said we'd test for recognition of the appropriate responses to the five types of resistance. How might you modify the question to test for both dimensions of the objective?

Pete   It looks to me as though we could do it with a matching test item. On the left we'd have the ten items, only five of which would be indicators. On the right we'd have descriptions of responses to resistance.

You said something the other day about one question giving away the answer to another question—something to avoid. It seems that if we only put five response descriptions on the right, they might provide clues to the five indicators on the left. So I think I'd put more than five response descriptions on the right— add some distracters. Then the likelihood of participants getting the question right by chance is reduced a lot.

Mary   I think that would do it. You analyzed that very well. And I'm pleased that you remembered our discussion about the challenge of developing effective test questions. That's a task you'll soon need to undertake for your program. Because you need to develop the test for Level 2 evaluation after you develop your objectives—but before you develop the training program.

There's another important point. We want to know that it is the training program that's responsible for participants achieving the objectives. So we need a before-program measure. If we don't administer a pretest, we will miss the possibility that participants could have achieved the objectives before training.

Pete Now I understand why you were saying that we need to plan for program evaluation while we are planning for program development.

Mary That's right. Now, to help you get ready for developing the test for learning, I'm going to give you this book, *Criterion-Referenced Test Development*, by Sharon A. Shrock and William C.C. Coscarelli. It's one of the better ones I know of. It's scholarly without being complicated, and it will give you the right foundation.

Level 3: Applying Learning

Pete So what about Level 3 evaluation—applying learning to the job?

Mary Now we're getting to your ultimate objectives—ensuring that the training has had a positive influence on job performance. Unfortunately, many trainers completely ignore this evaluation level. They seem to assume that the logic that led to their training design is good enough to ensure that the desired results are happening on the job.

But that's a shaky assumption. And it's even worse than it sounds, because many trainers never bother with Level 2 measurement, either. The only data they have are from their Level 1 evaluations. So the trainers can't even tell whether participants actually learned what they were supposed to—let alone whether they are applying what they learned on the job.

So what would you do? How would you evaluate your training program at Kirkpatrick's third level?

Pete I guess I'd ask the training participants whether they're using what they learned. I'd ask them to describe to me what they do differently now, compared to what they did before they went through the training. I'd ask for specific examples of how they are applying the knowledge and skills they learned in the training program.

Mary Do you see any limitations in asking the participants themselves how they are using what they learned?

Pete I suppose they might be biased. They might even want to look good or make me or the interviewer feel good. That could bias the data.

To overcome that bias, I could talk to their managers. I suppose I could also watch the training participants doing their jobs. But that might be harder to pull off.

Mary One thing to remember is that you're trying to get a handle on changes in performance that might be attributable to the training. Unless you have a "before" performance measure, sometimes referred to as a baseline measure, it would be difficult to find out whether the "after" performance you observe is different.

Pete So if we want to do the Level 3 evaluation properly, we should gather baseline measures before people attend the training program—just like giving those pretests in order to make Level 2 evaluation meaningful.

Mary Right. And that brings us back to the importance of planning the evaluation of a program during the program-development process.

Your idea of talking to those who have participated in the training and to their managers is a good one. One-on-one interviews—face-to-face—probably give us the most useful information. But sometimes they aren't practical. The people we want to talk to may be spread out geographically. Or individual interviews may take too much time. One reason Level 3 evaluation is performed so seldom is that it can be costly to gather the information.

Questionnaires can help us reduce the cost of Level 3 evaluation. They require careful design. If you choose the questionnaire approach, you'll have to get someone involved who is experienced in questionnaire design. You may have to make some follow-up telephone calls to participants, as well. Telephone interviews aren't as effective as face-to-face interviews, but they can be more cost-effective.

Focus groups are also useful for gathering information. They can provide information more efficiently than individual interviews. We won't explore at this time all the factors to consider in using focus groups. Let me just say that this technique also requires specialized experience.

Some people think that Level 3 evaluation is unnecessary. They say we need only to focus on whether we are getting on-the-job results—Level 4. But that idea overlooks a crucial fact: If we didn't have a Level 3 measure, we wouldn't know the reason behind a lack of results on the job. It could result from trainees' failure to learn what was intended. But it could also result from something going on in the work environment.

When you plan your information-gathering activities for Level 3 evaluation, you'll need to take into account possible factors in the job environment that could prevent the application of newly learned knowledge and skill. All too frequently, we hear comments like this from the supervisors of newly trained employees: "I know that's what they taught you. Now I'm going to show you how we really do it."

If trainees don't receive proper, on-the-job reinforcement of what they learned in the formal training program, then we've wasted most or all of our investment in training.

Level 4: Measuring Results from Training

Mary   A lot of specialized knowledge and skill goes into developing evaluation strategies. And the greatest challenge of all is figuring out how to perform Level 4 evaluation. In Level 4 evaluation, we're interested in business results. What effect does the program have on measures that are important to the business? For example:

- Reduced employee turnover
- Reduced costs
- Improved quality
- Increases in favorable comments from customers
- Increased sales
- Fewer grievances filed; for example, harassment complaints
- Increased profitability

Pete   It seems like a pretty big leap from learning in the classroom to results in the real world. Can we really tell whether it was training that succeeded — or failed — when a change in results occurs?

Mary   That's the big question. In many cases, we can't tell without a great deal of research. That may involve a considerable investment of time and money. So many training directors judge that the benefits of Level 4 evaluation are not great enough to justify the investment required.

Pete   So Level 4 evaluation isn't practical?

Mary   It can be. In some settings, the business results may be simple to measure. For example, say that we observe a significant increase in sales and profitability after sales training. If other factors have been held constant, then we have strong evidence that the training was responsible for the gains.

Or say that we provide advanced training to some machine operators in how to minimize scrap. If we then observe a reduction in the amount and cost of scrap from those operators, then we have good evidence that the training was at least a major contributor to the result.

Pete   Why the hedge? Isn't it obvious that training was the factor that caused the result?

Mary   Unless we conduct a carefully designed study, using experimental and control groups, we have to recognize the possibility that other variables could have contributed to the result. We need to think in terms of evidence, not proof. We have evidence that training influenced the result. But we cannot state positively that training was the sole cause.

The examples I've given are simple ones. Measuring the effects of, say, supervisory or management training becomes much more difficult. Frequently, the skills participants learn in supervisory training programs are not reinforced in the workplace. After training, a supervisor may return to a job in which she or he works for a manager who does not have the skills.

In such instances we could say there's a lack of congruence between formal training and the workplace. It is somewhat like taking golf lessons when the game to be played is baseball. In general, organizations need to do a better job of connecting formal training to the work environment.

Pete   Mary, I appreciate the short course in evaluation. I know I have a lot to learn. But I think I have a better understanding now — at least of evaluation fundamentals. I'm looking forward to talking with you about how we can apply formative evaluation to the program as we develop it.

Index

Donald L. Kirkpatrick is Professor Emeritus, University of Wisconsin, and a widely respected teacher, author, and consultant. He has over thirty years of experience as professor of management at the University of Wisconsin and has held professional training and human resource positions with International Minerals and Chemical Corporation and Bendix Corporation. He is the author of eight management inventories and five books: *How to Manage Change Effectively, How to Improve Performance Through Appraisal and Coaching, How to Train and Develop Supervisors, How to Plan and Conduct Productive Business Meetings,* and *No-Nonsense Communication.* The first two titles received the "Best Book of the Year" award from the Society for Human Resource Management. Kirkpatrick is past president of the American Society for Training and Development and is best known for developing the internationally accepted four-level approach for evaluating training programs. He received his B.B.A., M.B.A., and Ph.D. degrees from the University of Wisconsin, Madison. He lives in Elm Grove, Wisconsin, and is a senior elder at Elmbrook Church and an active member of Gideons International.